The Inuit
and
Their Land

The Inuit
and
Their Land

The Story of Nunavut

Donald Purich

James Lorimer & Company, Publishers
Toronto, 1992

Cover photos: R. Freeman, Tessa Macintosh

Canadian Cataloguing in Publication Data

Purich, Donald J., 1947-
   The Inuit and their land

Includes index.
ISBN 1-55028-383-9 (bound). ISBN 1-55028-382-0 (pbk.)

1. Inuit - Northwest Territories - Claims.
    2. Inuit - Northwest Territories - Land transfers.
    3. Inuit - Northwest Territories - Land tenure.
    4. Inuit - Canada - Government relations.
    5. Nunavut (N.W.T.). I. Title.
E99.E7P87 1992 323.1'1971 C92-093756-X

James Lorimer & Company, Publishers
Egerton Ryerson Memorial Building
35 Britain Street
Toronto, Ontario
M5A 1R7

Printed in Canada

Contents

Acknowledgements

A number of people and institutions were most helpful to me in preparing this book.

The Canada Council provided me with a travel grant which enabled me to visit several Arctic communities to interview people and carry out research. Curtis Fahey, former trade editor at James Lorimer & Co., Richard Bartlett and Howard McConnell, both from the College of Law at the University of Saskatchewan, were kind enough to write letters supporting my grant application to the Council.

The College of Law at the University of Saskatchewan provided me with a six-month leave from my duties as director of the Native Law Centre to work on the book and also provided me with some funds for travel expenses connected with the book. I am especially grateful to Dean Peter MacKinnon for helping me obtain both.

Sandy Harris, Research Officer, Marie Doyle, Research Assistant and Alan Downe, Director, all of the Office of Research Services of the Northwest Territories Legislative Assembly, were most helpful in finding NWT government documents for me. Lynda Chambers, who served as editor and librarian at the Tungavik Federation of Nunavut office in Ottawa, provided me with various documents and information relating to the Inuit land claim. Both the Department of Indian Affairs and Canadian Arctic Resources Committee in Ottawa gave me access to their libraries and photocopy machines.

Maliiganik Tukisiiniakvik (the legal aid service based in Iqaluit) granted me access to some of their files dealing with justice and social issues in the eastern Arctic. Its director, Neil Sharkey, was particularly helpful. Nunatta campus of Arctic College gave me access to their library, whose northern collection was particularly valuable. The archives staff at the Prince of Wales Northern Heritage Centre in Yellowknife were also helpful in finding a number of archival items for me.

I am particularly grateful to Neil Sharkey and Anne Crawford for their hospitality when I visited Iqaluit.

My editor at James Lorimer & Co., Diane Young, provided a number of excellent suggestions for improving the content and flow of the manuscript.

A great number of people in both northern and southern Canada spoke to me about various specific issues relating to the book. I have acknowledged their assistance in my list of sources appearing at the end of the book.

I would also like to acknowledge the contribution that a great many students in the Program of Legal Studies for Native People have made to my better understanding of Aboriginal issues. Aboriginal students from all across Canada seek information on, apply to and attend that program. The goal of the program is to increase the number of Aboriginal students in law school. In the eleven years that I have run the program as Director of the Native Law Centre I have learned a lot from those students about Aboriginal issues, culture and views. The students who have come from the NWT, northern Quebec and Labrador have been most helpful in my understanding some of the issues discussed in this book.

While a lot of people have assisted me, all the opinions and judgments are my own. And so are the errors, which I hope are few.

Finally, I would like to dedicate this book to my wife Karen Bolstad in appreciation of her patience as I worked on the manuscript and to my son Nicholas who always wanted to know "are you doing more typing, daddy?" and "will there be more paper coming out of the machine?"

Introduction

These are exciting times in Canada. The country is being redefined, and that redefinition involves more than Quebec's relationship with the rest of Canada. While the country focuses on its relationship with Quebec, equally exciting developments are occurring in Canada's north. There the majority Aboriginal[1] population is struggling to develop home rule through various means, including control of the legislative assembly, devolution of authority to the territorial government and the land claims process. At the same time, there is a push by the Northwest Territories' seventeen thousand Inuit to divide the Territories and form their own territory, Nunavut, out of the eastern half.

Since 1980 support for division and the establishment of Nunavut has come from both the federal and territorial governments. A land claims agreement-in-principle between Ottawa and the Inuit signed in Igloolik on April 30, 1990, included a statement by the federal government that it supported in principle the creation of Nunavut. In mid-October 1990 the Inuit leader, Paul Quassa, and territorial government leader Dennis Patterson signed a joint letter to the prime minister calling for legislation dividing the territory when the land claims agreement becomes final and the establishment of the government of Nunavut five years after that division.

As this book was being completed in early 1992 there were even more exciting developments on the horizon. A non-binding vote was held, approving by a small majority a possible boundary line between the two new territories. The Inuit agreement had been finalized. Unfortunately, at the time of writing, the text of the final agreement had not yet been made

---

1 In recent years, Aboriginal scholars and writers have argued that words like *Aboriginal*, *Native* and *Indigenous* should be capitalized because they refer to specific groups of Canadians. I agree with this and hence throughout this book I have capitalized these words.

public, though it was said by parties involved that it did not differ significantly from the 1990 agreement-in-principle. According to my sources, the final agreement provided some of the details that had not been worked out earlier and also dealt with a number of legal technicalities. Tentatively, the vote to ratify the final agreement was scheduled for early fall, 1992. Assuming a positive vote on the land claims agreement, the federal government undertook to introduce legislation to divide the territory and have Nunavut become reality towards the end of the decade.

At the same time there was yet another round of major constitutional discussions. The outcome of those was unpredictable, but it became clear during the winter of 1992 that Aboriginal issues would be a major part of any new constitutional deal. It was also clear that there was considerable support for the entrenchment of Aboriginal self-government in the constitution and a recognition that this right was an inherent one. However, public support for the entrenchment of the inherent right of self-government seemed to be on the understanding that such rights be exercised within the limits of the Canadian constitution.

While there was uncertainty as to the outcomes of both sets of discussions, some things can be said to be certain. The Inuit will continue their quest for Nunavut. In my view, a negative vote on the land claim agreement will only delay the creation of Nunavut. The reasons for its creation will remain. And at some point the territories will be divided.

It is also certain that, however the vote goes, the agreement will continue to be seen as an important document because it includes many of the principles that the Inuit have argued for in the last twenty years. The comments in this book about the Inuit land claim are based on the 1990 agreement-in-principle and on what I have learned of this final agreement. These same principles will undoubtedly be included in any future re-negotiated agreement.

Nunavut can come into being in two ways. The Inuit can simply declare their independence, an unrealistic alternative given current economic and political realities and a position that Inuit leaders have rejected, or Nunavut can be established through negotiation with southern Canada. If Nunavut comes to fruition as a result of the current negotiations, in ten to twenty years the result will be a province run and controlled by Inuit, where Inuktitut will be the language of the government and where Inuit concerns will be the dominant ones. While the Inuit have insisted that this proposed government will be a public one, serving the interests of all the eastern Arctic's people, in reality, with over 80 percent of the area's population of Inuit origin the government cannot help but be an ethnic one. The redefined Canada that emerges after the current constitutional showdown will then have two governments with ethnic majorities other than Anglo-Canadian, those of Quebec and Nunavut.

Nunavut's ethnic composition may well mean enshrining a third language and culture in Canada's constitution. The development of Nunavut will require understanding and tolerance on the part of southern Canadians for this reason and for others. Nunavut will need significant federal financial support—at a time of financial restraint—to make it viable. Current economic realities are such that in the immediate future Nunavut will not be financially self-sufficient and will have to be supported by southern Canada to a greater extent than any have-not province. At the same time, decisions on northern resource development will have to take into account not only southern needs but the needs and wishes of the people of the north. Even the creation of the province of Nunavut will need the legal blessing of southern Canadians. Based on Canada's current constitution, seven provinces with at least 50 percent of the country's population will have to consent if Nunavut is to evolve into provincehood or into something like an autonomous territory.

The evolution of Nunavut may also have an impact on the development of the new Quebec-Canada relationship. A significant portion of northern Quebec is in fact Inuit territory, home to more than six thousand Inuit. Legally, northern Quebec only became part of that province in 1912. Might the Inuit of northern Quebec seek someday to affiliate with Nunavut? Can they, for instance, claim that their surrender of Aboriginal title in the 1975 James Bay Agreement was on the understanding that Quebec remain a province within the Canadian federation on the current terms?

The same can be said of the Newfoundland-Canada relationship. The Inuit in Labrador, who at the time of writing were engaged in negotiations to settle their land claim, probably have more in common with their cultural kin in Nunavut then they do with most Newfoundlanders. The development of Nunavut may well cause Newfoundland to redefine its relationship with some of its people.

While southern Canadians have an important stake in Nunavut, the north remains a mystery to most Canadians, and that in spite of the tax dollars the Canadian government has put into asserting Canadian sovereignty in the Arctic. One Canadian author, Peter Cumming, an Osgoode Hall law professor who has worked extensively with Inuit organizations as a legal adviser, estimated that fewer than 5 percent of Canadians have actually travelled in the north. "Is there really such a place as Inuvik?" a Saskatoon cab driver asked me as I returned from a trip there. In view of the implications Nunavut has for the rest of Canada, Canadians owe it to themselves to become informed about developments taking place in northern Canada.

For example, as Nunavut becomes reality, Canadians can learn lessons that may help build a better relationship with Aboriginal people in the rest of the country. Nunavut may be the key development that will convince Canadians that we can build a pluralistic society in which Aboriginal people play an important role. As executive federalism (wherein decisions are increasingly being made by federal and provincial first ministers) grows in importance, a first minister representing an Aboriginal province may well force Canadians to rethink their view of their country.

In writing this book I am mindful of the criticism that has often, and on occasion correctly, in my view, been levelled at southern-based journalists and academics.

There is a school of thought that wants to "pickle Eskimo society," complained Quebec Inuit leader Mark Gordon at a 1985 Montreal conference marking the tenth anniversary of the signing of the James Bay Agreement. These people "haven't been in the North long enough to get frostbite." His complaint is one echoed by many Inuit and northerners. Southern writers, journalists, academics and governments have defined and dominated the discussion relating to northern development. Control of the northern political agenda by southern Canadians and control of Inuit life by non-Inuit southerners is one of the reasons the Inuit seek their own government.

This book is not an attempt to tell southern Canada about the north. That is something Inuit people and northerners must do themselves. Rather, this book is an attempt to sensitize Canadians to the major issues Canada will have to face as Canada's Inuit work towards building Nunavut. It is a follow-up to my two earlier books, *Our Land* and *The Metis*, and it attempts to place the unique claim of the Inuit into a wider national context. In a way, what the Inuit seek is not much different from the goals and aspirations of other Aboriginal peoples. What is unique in their claim is that they are by far the majority of the population in the land they occupy and as a result their demand for self-government is much more politically acceptable to a great many Canadians.

That is, in part, why I assume that in one form or another Nunavut will become reality in the next ten to twenty years. Nunavut faces serious practical obstacles, especially economic ones. But the quest for Nunavut is more than mere words and numbers. It is a dream and an emotion similar to the nationalism in Quebec or the francophone drive for protection in Canada. The dream of Nunavut is one which is not going to be forgotten or forsaken.

Of course, the division of the territories will be a heart-wrenching exercise. There are many northerners, and some southerners, who passionately believe that such a division is a mistake. To put it into a southern context, for some people the emotional impact of dividing the Northwest Territories will be like dividing Ontario between south and north, or like separating the Fraser Delta from the rest of British Columbia. And perhaps for this reason initially the break might not be a total one, but might involve the formation of two strong regional governments under a territorial umbrella.

Nevertheless, in the long term Nunavut will become part of Canada's future political reality. It will evolve into a province and will adopt a role as protector of Inuit culture and language. This will mean an evolution of the Canadian federation to accommodate an Aboriginal society as part of the Canadian mainstream.

1

Setting the Stage

A Future Scenario: A.D. 2020

The year 2020 has been one of the toughest Canadian winters on record. Vancouver has had four snowfalls in one month, one snowfall reaching a record 40 centimetres with temperatures near -10°C. Toronto was virtually shut down for a week, as a massive snow storm dumped over 100 centimetres of snow in three days and an accompanying cold front dropped temperatures into the -20s. Nor has the rest of Canada been spared.

The record cold temperatures have seriously tested Canada's energy supply. At the height of the cold spell a consortium of Canadian and American companies has announced a plan to bring northern gas and oil south. The plan is to ship natural gas, which has been liquefied in a plant at Bathurst Island in the high Arctic, south in transport submarines, along with oil from the area.

The idea is not new. In 1977 a Canadian consortium announced a plan that involved liquefying natural gas on Melville Island and shipping it south through Lancaster Sound in two giant tankers. A similar scenario was floated in January 1990, except that it involved transporting oil instead of gas by submarine tanker from Lougheed Island in the high Arctic. Like many other schemes involving Arctic hydrocarbons, it too created a flurry of activity and was then shelved.

The day of transforming the dream into reality has come in 2020. Canada needs the energy. As southern Canadians shiver in the below normal temperatures, the federal government has declared its support for the proposal.

Understandably, northerners are less than enthusiastic about the proposal. Having submarine tankers filled with natural gas and oil represents a serious threat to their lifestyle, to say nothing of the potential environmental threat.

Their government, Nunavut, has passed tough energy conservation and taxation legislation limiting the number of drilling permits that can be issued and imposing a heavy tax on oil and gas production, making both uneconomical. Critics of the Nunavut government say that those measures had nothing to do with energy conservation, but rather were an attempt to block oil and gas shipment through the environmentally sensitive Lancaster Sound, between Baffin and Devon islands. The area is rich in animal life needed to support traditional lifestyles, including whales who use sound waves to communicate. Their communications would be disrupted by the submarines. Under Canada's constitution, control over shipping rests with the federal government. Nunavut could not directly ban the submarine traffic, therefore, but it does have the power to control resource development.

In an editorial, *The Globe and Mail* asked: "Should 40,000 Inuit Hold 35 Million Canadians Hostage?" The bilingual (Inuktitut and English) *Nunatsiaq News*, published in Iqaluit, has responded with a slogan reminiscent of one emanating from Alberta in the 1970s: "Let the Southerners Freeze." The article goes on to point out that in 1982 southern Canadians agreed to a new constitution which clearly confirmed provincial jurisdiction over "exploration for non-renewable natural resources" and over "development, conservation and management of non-renewable natural resources ... including ... the rate of primary production therefrom...."

In the midst of the crisis, the Nunavut Legislative Assembly is in session. The twenty-five-member assembly is sitting as the Interprovincial Relations Committee of the Whole, listening to views of northerners. The proceedings are in Inuktitut, with simultaneous translation into English and French for the four members who are not Inuit.

The committee is listening to a presentation from the Hunters' and Trappers' Association of Pond Inlet, a community of 1,200 near the northern end of Baffin Island. The giant transport submarines will pass within one hundred kilometres of that community. The presentation is being made via a two-way television hookup, which links the Legislative Assembly to twenty-eight other Arctic communities as well. Not only are the proceedings being broadcast into the communities, but residents of those communities are allowed to ask questions and voice their views during the presentation.

The committee meeting is taking place in the igloo-shaped Assembly Building in the capital, Iqaluit. The Assembly Building sits on a hill overlooking the rest of the town.

Like Nunavut, Iqaluit has flourished. While the government has operated in a decentralized way, Iqaluit still remains the most significant centre in the eastern Arctic.

Work has been underway for nearly two decades to bring the above scenario to reality. While many of the details remain to be worked out both through negotiation with Ottawa and the territorial government and in consultation with Inuit communities, enough general principles have emerged that a portrait of Nunavut can be drawn with some accuracy. Since the early 1970s the Inuit, through their various organizations—the Inuit Tapirisat of Canada (ITC), the Nunavut Constitutional Forum (NCF) and the Tungavik Federation of Nunavut (TFN)—have defined how their future government will operate. The concept of Nunavut has been part and parcel of the Inuit land claim ever since they first put forward their land claim in 1976. The Inuit position has always been that before they sign a land claims agreement they must have a guarantee that Nunavut will be created.

What is Nunavut?

The Inuit have proposed that a new territory called Nunavut be created out of the central and eastern part of the Northwest Territories. Its government would be responsible for the estimated twenty-one thousand people living in this region. Eventually, its proponents hope, it would become a province. Of course, Nunavut is more than a government-in-waiting. It is a dream and a political ideal through which the Inuit hope to solve many of their problems and build a better future.

Its geographic area would be all of the current NWT north of the treeline. That line begins at the midway point of Manitoba's northern boundary and proceeds diagonally across the NWT to the area just north of Inuvik. Nunavut would still be Canada's largest territory and eventually province—covering approximately one-fifth of Canada's area—and in a region where the only means of transportation is air travel and, in the summer, ship. There are no highways in the eastern Arctic.

As things currently stand, the Mackenzie Delta–Beaufort Sea area, which is home to the Inuvialuit (as the Inuit people of the area are known), would not be part of Nunavut. Excluded would be six communities—Inuvik, Aklavik, Paulatuk, Tuktoyaktuk, Holman and Sachs Harbour—with significant Inuit populations, and portions of Victoria Island, Melville Island, all of Banks Island and several other smaller islands. As documented in Chapter Five, the exact location of the boundary has been one of the major stumbling blocks to the creation of Nunavut.

There would be approximately thirty communities in Nunavut, with almost all having a significant Inuit majority and half being north of the Arctic Circle. The largest community is Iqaluit—formerly Frobisher Bay—with a population of 3,500, followed by Rankin Inlet with a population of 1,500. The only major non-Inuit community in the eastern Arctic is the mining town of Nanisivik, at the northern tip of Baffin Island.

Government

While Nunavut would have a public government serving all its residents, it would have many unique characteristics. Because some 80 percent of the population of the eastern Arctic is Inuit, amounting to seventeen thousand people, the government of Nunavut would effectively serve the Inuit. Like Quebec, it would be a distinct society and would have a role, a *de facto* if not a legal role, in preserving Inuit culture and the Inuit language, Inuktitut.

Like other territories and provinces, Nunavut would have a legislative assembly, but because of the unique nature of the territory there would be some differences. One proposal floated in the mid-1980s suggested a twenty-five-member assembly with nine members elected on the basis of population and four seats guaranteed to each of the four regions: Beaufort Sea, Kitikmeot, Keewatin and Baffin. (As indicated earlier, however, the Beaufort area will probably not be part of Nunavut.) The issue of regional representation in the legislative assembly has plagued many jurisdictions; it is especially acute in the north where the strict application of proportional representation would mean that some small communities would find themselves represented by an MLA whose constituency covers thousands of square kilometres. In a recent court challenge to Saskatchewan's electorial boundaries, which favoured rural over urban areas, the Supreme Court in a majority judgment upheld such a distribution on the grounds that geographic considerations and the need for regional representation were valid factors to consider in drawing electoral boundaries.

Controversial proposals made in the mid-1980s suggested lengthy residency requirements, varying from three years to ten years, for a person to be eligible to vote. These proposals grew out of concern about the influence of southerners. The 1983 Nunavut Constitutional Forum (NCF) proposal looked at the impact of transient workers and reviewed schemes in the Shetlands (where transients are restricted to operational bases) and Greenland (where labour permits are required by migrant workers) as a way of having some control over the demographic make-up of the north. At the same time the paper recognized that moves to control southerners moving to Nunavut may well contravene Canada's Charter of Rights and Freedoms, which guarantees Canadians mobility rights and the right to work in all areas of the country.

Another contentious issue is the site of the capital of the new territory. The 1983 position paper prepared by the NCF recommended that the choice of the capital be deferred and that a constitutional conference select a location as its final piece of business. However, the location of the capital might not be as important as it has been in other jurisdictions. In Nunavut, communities would be given extensive powers and government would be decentralized. The 1987 Iqaluit agreement on division of the Northwest Territories between the NCF and its western counterpart, the Western Constitutional Forum (WCF), speaks of the importance of strong regional authorities which will reflect the role of communities in Inuit life. Regional government and decentralization are also important because such decentralization makes it easier to hire qualified Inuit personnel for government functions. It would allow many qualified Inuit to work for the government while remaining in their home communities. In a January 1992 meeting of Tungavik Federation of Nunavut (TFN) leaders and MLAs from the eastern Arctic, former government leader Dennis Patterson put forward the suggestion of one centre serving as the legislative capital, another centre as the administrative capital and yet another as the judicial capital.

Culture

Nunavut would have three official languages: Inuktitut, English and French. Inuktitut as the language of the government of Nunavut would give Inuit people an important advantage in running their government. Presumably the number of non-Inuit professionals and administrators who are fluent in Inuktitut is limited; therefore, Inuit people would likely fill most government posts. As Peter Ernerk, the former MLA for Aivilik, said, "There's not much point in having Nunavut if we have to hire southern professionals and administrators to run the government."

A Nunavut government would have an important role in protecting Inuit culture. That would mean recognition of and protection for Inuit customary law. Inuit customary law, like the customary law of Canada's other Aboriginal people, bears many similarities to English common law, upon which much of Canada's legal system is based. In essence, customary law is a system of unwritten rules for dealing with conflict. Like English common law, customary law is presumed to be understood by all the community and represent a community's consensus on dealing with unacceptable conduct. To a great many Inuit people, traditional rules for dealing with community offenders and family issues make a lot more sense than rules imposed from outside. The most likely application of customary law would be in the areas of family law, criminal law and civil disputes. Its application is not something that is totally foreign to the Canadian legal system. Already customary law has been working its way into the northern legal system. Decisions made in 1961 recognizing customary marriage and adoption practices opened the door to recognition of Inuit custom in various aspects of the legal system, including policing and sentencing of offenders.

On the assumption that an Inuit-controlled police force would be more willing than a federal force to apply Inuit custom as part of law enforcement, the 1976 Inuit Tapirisat of Canada (ITC) proposal spoke of establishing a Nunavut Police Force, just as Ontario and Quebec have their own provincial forces.

Cultural protection, of course, means more than language and customary law. It means a role in areas like broadcasting, a frequent source of contention between Ottawa and the provinces. The 1983 NCF paper spoke of the pioneering work of the Inuit Broadcasting Corporation and called for co-operation with the federal government in developing a communications plan for Nunavut. Protecting culture also means control over cultural sites and research in the north. "Too often research has been conducted with little regard for the needs and sensitivities of the people of Nunavut," complained the 1983 NCF paper.

As Nunavut is developed, constitutional guarantees might be included to protect Inuktitut and the role of Inuit people in government in the event there should be mass migration northward and the Inuit become a minority in Nunavut.

However, at the same time the Inuit have stressed that the rights of non-Inuit will be protected. The 1983 position paper spoke of a bill of rights to guarantee the rights of the non-Inuit minority. The 1987 Iqaluit agreement between the NCF and the WCF on division of the Northwest Territories spoke of guaranteeing to all non-Inuit "opportunities for personal fulfillment and social and political life."

Nunavut today is really a process, a process of negotiation and community consultation, out of which a new territory and eventually province will arise. The form of government has yet to be worked out. What Paul Quassa, the former journalist from Igloolik who signed the agreement-in-principle on the Inuit land claim as TFN president, sees as most important is that a process be established by which the government can be developed.

The Timetable for Nunavut

There is even a timetable for the establishment of Nunavut. While the idea of dividing the territory has been around for some time, the most recent thrust arises directly from the Inuit land claim. Since the early 1970s the Inuit have argued that settlement of their land claim and creation of Nunavut are linked and have to be negotiated at the same time. Initially the federal government disagreed and as a result the Inuit encountered considerable delay in advancing their land claim.

An important step was taken with the signing of the agreement-in-principle on the Inuit land claim. That agreement, signed in Igloolik on April 30, 1990, by the TFN and the federal and provincial governments, announced: "Consistent with their long-standing positions, the Government of Canada, the Territorial Government and the Tungavik Federation of Nunavut support in principle the creation of a Nunavut Territory, and the financing of a Nunavut government, outside of the claims agreement, as soon as possible." The agreement went on to state: "The Territorial Government and TFN undertake to develop, within six months of the Agreement, a process for giving effect to section 4.1.1 [the above section]." That agreement was a major breakthrough because Ottawa agreed to include provisions about the creation of Nunavut in a land claims agreement.

Paul Quassa, during his term as TFN president, stated that the goal for the creation of Nunavut is five years from the time the final land claims agreement is signed. That agreement was finalized in early 1992, a few months later than provided for in the agreement-in-principle. This would mean that Nunavut would come into being—initially as a territory rather than a province—sometime after 1997.

That five-year timetable for the creation of Nunavut was reiterated in the joint letter from the NWT government leader and the TFN president to Prime Minister Brian Mulroney dated October 19, 1990. Dennis Patterson, at the time government leader in the NWT, and Paul Quassa told Prime Minister Mulroney

> ... we are proposing that Canada agree to introduce legislation to Parliament creating a Nunavut Territory on or before the time the Nunavut land claims ratification legislation is expected to be introduced.... We foresee that legislation establishing a Nunavut Territory would stipulate that its substantive provisions would not come into effect until the fifth anniversary of its enactment. The five year period would allow the residents of the western part

of the Northwest Territories an opportunity to define new constitutional arrangements for their area.

The federal government responded in a guarded fashion, but subsequently, in negotiations leading to the agreement-in-principle, agreed to introduce legislation by the fall of 1992 to create Nunavut, with the territory to come into being later in the decade. Such legislation was subject to approval of the boundary by territorial residents—the concept was approved in a 1982 plebiscite and was called for in the 1990 agreement-in-principle—and to the Inuit ratifying their land claims agreement.

A territory-wide plebiscite on the boundary—not a binding referendum—was held on May 4, 1992, with 54 percent of ballots cast in favour of the proposed boundary. Ratification by the Inuit of the land claims agreement was tentatively slated for early November 1992. If the outcome of both votes is positive, the federal government would go ahead with its legislation to create Nunavut.

The TFN and the territorial and federal governments agreed to negotiate a political accord in the spring of 1992 that would outline what would be included in this federal legislation. A great many details will have to be worked out as the administration of the territory is divided among its two halves. Currently, there is no major eastern administrative centre: all of the territory is administered from Yellowknife. A Nunavut implementation and transition commission, scheduled to be set up in the fall of 1992, will decide on these details and others.

Earlier on, Paul Quassa had conceded that it may take up to ten years to put Nunavut into place, instead of the five years provided for in the timetable. In their January 1992 meeting in Iqaluit, Inuit leaders decided that the start-up date for Nunavut and the election of the first Nunavut Assembly should be moved to 1999 from 1997. Their goal was for the government to be fully operational by 2007.

Of course, even if the federal government proceeds with its legislation there are still obstacles which could derail Nunavut. These include financial issues and the possibility of an uncooperative territorial government or a federal government that changes its mind. A court order is another possible obstacle. Currently the Dene of northern Saskatchewan are suing for a declaration that some of Nunavut represents their traditional treaty and Aboriginal lands. In the aftermath of the vote approving the boundary, some Dene in the NWT have also threatened court intervention to block the division.

However, no matter what the outcome of the current initiative, it is clear that the Inuit are firmly committed to Nunavut. The concept of Nunavut has been something very close to the heart of the Inuit. Even if current initiatives falter, the push for Nunavut will go on.

The Reasons for Creating Nunavut

I believe that Nunavut is a dream; it is a dream of the Eastern Arctic people, the Inuit. It is a dream whose time has come to be realized.... There are many reasons for this dream to be realized ... A dream of ensuring Inuktitut as the main language in Nunavut Territory ... We dream of making laws and policies which truly reflect the needs and conditions of Nunavut Territory ...

Those were the words of Titus Allooloo, an Inuk MLA representing Igloolik and Hall Beach and a government minister, in the NWT Legislative Assembly on October 31, 1989.

The creation of Nunavut should be seen as a step in Canada's evolution. Historically, the Territories were never meant to be one political unit. It should be remembered that territories in Canada have traditionally been what has been left over after Ottawa has created provinces or parcelled off land to the provinces. In a sense, one could argue that the territorial government has been a political institution to park the leftover land still in Ottawa's hands while further constitutional development occurs. That development is the division of the Territories into Nunavut and a western territory.

The Inuit have advanced many arguments to support their contention that such constitutional development should occur and that it should lead to two new jurisdictions, one of them being Nunavut. The 1985 Nunavut Constitutional Forum position paper concluded:

We don't want a Nunavut government that is going to come in and tell us what to do. We have had enough of that already from the federal government and NWT governments, and from lots of other nice and helpful people who have come and gone. We don't want people, even the ones with best intentions, telling us what to do. We want to do it ourselves. That is what Nunavut is all about ...

It is not only because of mistreatment by first Ottawa and then Yellowknife that the Inuit seek their own government. For that matter, a strong case could be made that the present NWT government (hereafter referred to as the GNWT) has made a genuine and to some extent successful effort to incorporate Inuit into the government of the Northwest Territories. But perhaps the ethnic differences are too great. It goes without saying that Inuit culture and language are different from those of other residents of the NWT; these differences are readily visible even to the casual visitor. The differences are symbolized in things like the radio broadcasts in Inuktitut, the bilingual stop signs—Inuktitut and English—in Rankin Inlet, the bilingual *Nunatsiaq News* published in Iqaluit and circulating throughout the eastern Arctic, the Inuktitut signs in the Northern and Co-op stores throughout the eastern Arctic and the trilingual telephone book for the eastern Arctic, the first third of which is in Inuktitut. Such symbols alone are of course not an argument for an independent jurisdiction. However, culture and language can provide an important base on which a government can be built. And as in the case of Quebec, the Inuit believe they have a language and culture to protect and that only their own government can provide such protection. The predominance of Inuit in the eastern Arctic means that they have been more successful in retaining their language and culture than some southern Aboriginal nations.

So too, living above the treeline has an enormous psychological impact. To the Inuit there is something emotional about the treeless land, akin to what many prairie dwellers feel about the flat prairies. "I need to get out on the land and away from things," NWT MLA Peter Ernerk, the member for the Keewatin constituency of Aivilik, said in a 1990 interview. "Our people couldn't manage Ottawa or Calgary, because it's a different territory with trees etcetera, but we can manage our communities," he went on to say.

The history of the regions is also very different. The west has been dominated by the quest for resource development. Such pressures have not moulded the eastern Arctic. In a 1989 book commissioned by the TFN, *Nunavut: Political Choices and Manifest Destiny*, the four authors wrote:

> The Yellowknife government has subscribed to a vision in which southern Ontario values are imported into the North. In this vision, the aboriginal people will become increasingly compliant, and will abandon their puffery about aboriginal self-government and cultural rights....

Peter Ernerk put it this way: "They [the executive of the GNWT] can't really speak for the Inuit. It's an insult to think they can."

Distance is another argument advanced in favour of Nunavut. To the Inuit, Yellowknife is not their government. "Living in Baffin Island and having your government in Yellowknife is the equivalent of living in Montreal and having your capital in Regina. It is the equivalent of the premier of Alberta, Donald Getty, deciding language policy for the people of Quebec," John Amagoalik, co-chair of the Inuit Committee on National Issues, declared at a 1987 conference following that year's failed federal-provincial conference on Aboriginal rights. The distance from Iqaluit to Yellowknife is nearly 2,300 kilometres. (The distance from Montreal to Edmonton is approximately 2,800 kilometres.) Nor was it easy in the past to travel to Yellowknife from the eastern Arctic. Even today it is probably far easier to travel south from any point in the Territories than it is to travel east and west. In fact, until 1980 there was no scheduled east-west territorial air service. Anyone wanting to travel from Yellowknife to Frobisher Bay (as Iqaluit was known) had to travel via Montreal.

A government covering a smaller geographic area could be more efficient. As the Inuit Tapirisat's 1979 position paper, *Political Development in Nunavut*, pointed out, "Substantial transportation costs, always a significant factor in the North, could be saved by bringing government closer to the people."

Division is inevitable, a senior government official has said, there are too many differences between east and west. As Peter Ernerk put it, "The western MLAs want to talk about roads;

we don't care about roads because there are none in the eastern Arctic." And he talks about trees: "We wouldn't profess to run territory with all those trees, so why should outsiders come and run our territory?"

Yellowknife is no more home to the Inuit of the eastern Arctic than is Ottawa. The people of Nunavut are a distinct people with needs and aspirations of their own. For the Inuit of the eastern Arctic, therefore, the most compelling reason for creating Nunavut is home rule.

Nunavut and Aboriginal Self-Government

While the proposals for Nunavut, if implemented, will result in a unique government, and while the drive for Nunavut has been propelled by some factors unique to the north, it must also be seen as part of the drive by Canada's Aboriginal people for self-government. "Our right to govern the land we claim is a right we claim in our own right, and not as a special favour or grant," ITC president Rosemarie Kuptana told a parliamentary committee on the constitution in early January 1992. She, like many other Aboriginal leaders, insists that their right of self-government is inherent—that is has always existed and continues to exist no matter what governments say—and that the Nunavut land claims settlement does not mean that Inuit are giving up their rights to such governments. Traditionally, governments have viewed a land claims agreement as a way of extinguishing all Aboriginal rights.

Self-government essentially means the right of a community to govern its own affairs. It does not mean independence from Canada; rather, it means defining the terms under which an Aboriginal community is part of the larger federal state, much in the same way that some in Quebec are seeking to redefine that province's role within Canada. Aboriginal self-government means control over those matters of local interest that have a direct impact on daily lives, such as health care, education, economic development and justice. For the most part these are areas where the provinces currently exercise jurisdiction. Equally important, self-government means ensuring that those services are delivered by a civil service that is primarily Aboriginal.

Self-government means more than acting as an agent in the delivery of services for the federal or provincial government. That is known as devolution. While some Aboriginal communities have accepted such a devolution of powers, they have also sought something more, namely independent control over specific areas of jurisdiction without any restraints from other levels of government.

There are three main reasons for self-government. First, there is the natural desire of human beings to run their own affairs. Second, decisions made on behalf of Aboriginal people by other levels of government have not always been satisfactory, and because of that, Aboriginal people believe that they can administer their affairs better than can government officials. In the case of the Inuit as in the case of Indian people, it has to be remembered that for many years major decisions on services were made in Ottawa by bureaucrats and politicians who had little contact with the people. Finally, as many Aboriginal people see it, the alternative to self-government is assimilation, an option that has been rejected by most Aboriginal people.

The natural desire on the part of people to run their own affairs is not limited to Aboriginal people. It fuelled the decolonization drive in much of the Third World. It is evident as the Blacks of South Africa seek to change their country so they can have a say in the operations of the government, and it also became evident in the Soviet Union in the early 1990s as the peoples of the various constituent republics fought for freedom from control by the central government.

Canada has recognized the desire for self-determination by signing the International Covenant on Civil and Political Rights. The Covenant states:

> All peoples have the right of self-determination. By virtue of that right they freely determine their political status and freely pursue their economic, social and cultural development.

Canada restated its commitment in the Helsinki Accords of 1975, which reaffirmed the right to self-determination.

Canada's Aboriginal people have reminded the Canadian government of this international commitment. They argue that they have had the right to self-determination since time im-memorial. They point out that they governed themselves before the arrival of the Europeans and have never given up that right.

Not only is Aboriginal self-government an opportunity to exercise control over services in the best interests of the people themselves, it is more importantly an opportunity to preserve Aboriginal culture and language. It is the hope of many Aboriginal people that their government will use their language as the language of work, that it will make efforts to preserve their culture and that perhaps some cultural components will be incorporated in the government services. For example, many Aboriginal people hope that their customary way of dealing with disputes might in some way be incorporated into the delivery of justice, or that traditional healing concepts might be incorporated into the delivery of health care. And by using an Aboriginal language as the language of operation, the hope of many communities is that government administrative and service jobs might be filled by Aboriginal people, who because of their knowledge of the language will have an advantage in competing for such jobs.

Essential to the demands of Aboriginal people is constitutional protection for their future governments, to ensure that the powers of their governments can never be fettered or taken away by another government. This is the kind of constitutional protection provinces currently have against federal encroachment on their powers. Some have suggested that self-governing Aboriginal communities be given powers equivalent to those of municipalities. This would be insufficient, however. Municipal governments are creatures of the provincial legislature; their powers can be, and have been, taken away or changed by the provincial government without consent.

Having the financial resources to govern independently is another essential. Financing has been a major obstacle to the development of self-government. The financial situation of most Aboriginal communities is such that the only immediate realistic arrangement for financing such governments is transfer payments from other levels of government.

Four federal-provincial constitutional conferences were held between 1983 and 1987 with the aim of constitutionalizing the principle of Aboriginal self-government. Those conferences, as detailed in Chapter Six, ended in failure. Nonetheless, in a small way the move to self-government has continued. The official federal policy has been to devolve responsibility for Indian programs upon Indian bands and tribal councils. By the late 1980s well over half of the federal budget for services on Indian communities was being administered by the Indian bands and tribal councils. In some areas, such as education, Ottawa's powers have almost totally been turned over to the Indian nations.

In 1985, the federal Minister of Indian Affairs at the time, David Crombie, announced that the federal government would enter into negotiations with any band desiring greater control over its affairs. The 650-member Sechelt Band on the British Columbia coast was the first to take advantage of this offer. Since the announcement of the policy, 115 self-government proposals have been put forward by 285 bands, and the government has opened negotiations with over 30 different bands. In its 1988–89 annual report the Department of Indian Affairs stated:

> The Government of Canada is committed to the principle that Indian and Inuit communities wishing to govern themselves should do so.... This commitment to aboriginal self-government is a major focus of the department.

At the same time as Crombie was making his announcement, Peter Lougheed, who was then premier of Alberta, announced a plan to grant greater responsibility to the eight Métis settlements in that province. After several drafts of legislation were publicly discussed, legislation was passed in 1990 to implement Lougheed's plan. Among other powers granted to the Métis settlements is the power to define their own membership, a right Aboriginal communities have long sought. The Métis have also gained constitutional protection for the lands that make up the settlements.

None of these devolutions of powers has meant true self-government, because powers that are devolved can also be withdrawn. But they do represent part of a national trend to greater control of Aboriginal affairs by Aboriginal people. At the time of writing, discussions were ongoing to develop a new constitution for Canada. As documented later, there appeared in the spring of 1992 to be considerable support for entrenching the right of self-government in any new constitution.

Of course, there are some differences in what the Inuit seek in self-government and what other Aboriginal people seek. For the most part, the Inuit, be they in northern Quebec or the eastern Arctic, have looked to a public government to satisfy their aspirations for self-government. And in fact, Inuit spokespersons have often argued that what they are seeking is not self-government, but public government in which they will play a role appropriate to their numbers. The fact that the Inuit have chosen a public form of government rather than one which would serve Inuit people exclusively may well make it more palatable to non-Aboriginal communities.

The model of a public government, but one dominated by the Inuit, may reduce conflict with non-Aboriginal governments in another way as well. In the United States, tribal governments have fought extensive legal battles trying to assert their jurisdiction. If Nunavut is a province-like government, such jurisdictional disputes are much less likely, for such a government would be the beneficiary of decades of constitutional practice that had already settled the jurisdiction of provinces.

In approaching the question of self-government, it is important to remember that the Inuit, like other Aboriginal people, have been around a long time. And at one time, they were self-governing.

2

The Early History of Nunavut

We found about 20 intact house depressions at Gupuk ...
Gupuk was a very large settlement, perhaps with several
hundred people living in a dozen or more houses ... One
house was excavated ... Our excavations showed it to be
of the "cruciform" type which appears to have been
unique to the Siglit ... The floor and raised sleeping platforms were made from driftwood logs. The superstructure
was then covered with earth and sod to insulate it ...

This was how Charles Arnold, senior archaeologist at Yellowknife's Prince of Wales Heritage Centre, described the Inuit
community of Gupuk in the Mackenzie Delta in a 1988 *Northern Review* article.

Inuit people have occupied Canada's north for a long time.
Even where they were relative latecomers, as in the Mackenzie
Delta, their communities existed long before any European
settlements in the West. Like other Aboriginal people, the Inuit
were self-sufficient and self-governing before the Europeans
invaded their territory. While Aboriginal governments were
different from European governments, social organization and
control was a reality among the Inuit, as among other Aboriginal people.

Initially, the Europeans were content to leave the Inuit to
their ways. When Canada took over administration of the Arctic, its main preoccupation was with asserting sovereignty
over the territory; for the first forty years after Canada assumed jurisdiction over the north it acted as if the Inuit did
not exist. Commercialism, and later a desire by missionaries
and government to better the Inuit way of life, changed that.
At the same time, there was a belief in southern Canada that
all residents had to be taught to respect Canadian law, and that
the north had to be made safe for southern Canadians to ex-

plore. Inuit suddenly found themselves subject to a foreign standard when it came to resolving disputes.

Fur traders and missionaries established trading posts and missions. Eventually, settlements were built around them, increasing rapidly with the advent of well-meaning federal welfare measures. While such measures introduced many benefits to the Inuit, they also made many of the people into dependent wards of the state. It is this dependence that the Inuit are now trying to shake off.

The Arctic's First People

Archaeologists estimate that humans first crossed into the western hemisphere via a land bridge between Siberia and Alaska some 30,000 to 40,000 years ago (though some estimates have placed the first crossing as early as 100,000 years ago). As far as can be determined, these people did not stay in the Arctic.

The first evidence of Arctic settlement dates back some 4,000 years by people known as the Denbigh or Arctic Small Tool people, so named after the tools they left behind. According to Robert McGhee in *Canadian Arctic Prehistory*, they may have been Siberian neolithic people of the Chukchi Peninsula or Alaskan descendants of Micro-Blade people who crossed the land bridge about 8,000 years ago. They settled when the Arctic was warmer, and one theory states that they abandoned the Arctic and moved south as temperatures became colder.

The pre-Dorset followed. They occupied the area around Hudson Bay and the territory in the area of Hudson Strait and Foxe Basin between 3000 and 500 B.C. Pre-Dorset sites have been found as far south as Nain, Labrador, and as far west as the central NWT. McGhee estimates their population at between 1,000 and 3,000.

The Dorset people, known to the Inuit as the Tunit, followed. Between 1700 B.C. and A.D. 1000 they occupied the Arctic from the present site of Coppermine on the Arctic coast to Nain, Labrador, and Greenland in the east. They also occupied many of Canada's northern islands. McGhee suggests that they were probably the only occupants of Newfoundland's west coast between 500 B.C. and A.D. 500. He estimates their population between 2,000 and 5,000. There is evidence that they were the first people to build snowhouses, that they used sleds pulled by people and shaped bones for instruments and weapons. It is believed that they became extinct, perhaps because of an inability to adjust their lifestyle to a warming trend.

Temperatures reached a cold point sometime between 100 B.C. and 100 A.D., then warmed around 1000 A.D. to the extent that the treeline moved approximately 100 kilometres north. In 1200 A.D. the climate began to cool again, reaching a cold point sometime between 1600 and 1850.

The ancestors of today's Inuit are believed to be the Thule people—so-named after the place in Greenland where their ruins were first uncovered—who migrated from Alaska some 1,000 years ago. They were the last major migration of people into the Canadian Arctic. They distinguished themselves from their predecessors in that they hunted whales and used dogs, and chose coastal areas as their hunting and camping grounds. Even today, the Inuit remain a coastal people, with Baker Lake in central NWT being one of the few inland Inuit communities. The Thule people also used kayaks and umiaks, large open skin boats.

Lifestyle changed as temperatures dropped. The high Arctic islands, north of Barrow Strait, are believed to have been abandoned between A.D. 1300 and 1700. During this time, the people turned to seals and caribou as food sources, in addition to whales. Tents and igloos replaced stone and turf houses. The largest population concentrated in the Mackenzie Delta area because of its significant game resources.

Several significant settlements have been found in that area. Robert McGhee excavated several sites, the most important being Kittigazuit, west of modern-day Tuktoyaktuk. He estimates that it had a population of 1,000 and was the largest community between the Bering Sea and Greenland. Gupuk, across the river from Kittigazuit, was another major Inuit community, most likely abandoned in the mid-1800s.

Unfortunately, the Siglit, builders of these communities and probably the largest group of Arctic Inuit at the time of European contact, have largely vanished. Several anthropologists estimate their pre-contact population at 2,500, but by 1930 they numbered less than 200, the reduction attributed to disease introduced by the Europeans. Today, many Inuit in the

Delta area are Inupiat originating in Alaska who arrived in the 1920s. Some came looking for better hunting grounds. American whalers brought others to hunt caribou for them—although the Inupiat were whalers, a fact ignored by the Americans. The fact of this recent migration has prompted some people to suggest that the claim of the Inuvialuit (as the people are known today) to Aboriginal title is weak as they may not meet the test of occupation of the land since time immemorial. The federal government, however, has accepted the claim of the Inuvialuit and concluded an agreement based on that claim.

While the Mackenzie Delta area was the most populous, thanks to its comparatively mild climate and plentiful game, the Inuit used and occupied a significant portion of the rest of the Arctic. In Igloolik, for example, archaeologists trace constant settlement for some four thousand years. The three-volume 1976 Inuit Land Use and Occupancy Project found that the Inuit used all the land south of the northern arm of the Northwest Passage (starting in the west at McClure Strait, then proceeding through Viscount Melville Strait, Barrow Strait and finally Lancaster Sound) to the treeline and used some of the islands further to the north including Devon Island, the southern portion of Ellesmere Island, Cornwallis Island and the southeastern portion of Bathurst Island. The Inuit also used portions of northeastern Manitoba (a study published in a 1989 issue of the *Northern Review* estimated that some 12,000 square kilometres in Manitoba north of Churchill is traditional Inuit territory) and there is some evidence they may have also used the northeast corner of Saskatchewan into the nineteenth century.

Before contact with Europeans, the Inuit grouped themselves into extended families and hunting groups. Anthropologists believe that the traditional Inuit family had some five or six members. Families in turn joined hunting groups, usually made up of six to ten families, though when game was scarce the group might break into smaller units. These hunting groups would in turn share common ancestors with other members of the same dialect group or tribe. A tribe contained approximately five hundred people, and would be spread out over thousands of square kilometres of land and sea. Anthropologists estimate population density at one person per five hundred square kilometres.

The hunters, who were male, were responsible for passing on their skills to younger children. Groups had shamans whose responsibility was to act as intermediaries between the human world and the spiritual world.

For the most part, the Inuit depended upon whales, seals and walruses for food, though some Inuit also hunted caribou. Their dependence on wild game meant that they were a nomadic people. Winter travel was by dog team and komatik (sled) and summer travel was by foot. In summer, they lived in tents made of skin; winter housing included the renowned igloo, and homes of sod, whalebone and stone. A large structure was built in the fall where the community could hold festivities, singing and dancing, including the drum dance.

Decisions were made by consensus. Elder relatives exercised social control and authority. Everyone in the extended family knew who had control over them and over whom they had authority. When elders were unable to resolve a dispute, other forms of dispute resolution were resorted to, including song competitions and contests of strength such as wrestling and boxing. Gossip was another means of social control. If all else failed, persons considered a threat to the community were either executed or ostracized from the community.

In Aboriginal times, before contact with Europeans, Inuit lifestyles varied somewhat from area to area. The Ungava Inuit of northern Quebec and the Belcher Islands (in Hudson Bay) had some wood available to them; they relied on migratory birds for much of their diet. The south Baffin people often traded with their Ungava neighbours. The Salliq people of Southampton Island relied heavily on polar bear and walrus. Living in an area that in some years is ice-bound all year round, the Netsilik, who lived near King William Island, became particularly adept at hunting for seals on ice, while the Caribou Inuit of the interior Keewatin relied on caribou as their main source of food. The Mackenzie Inuit (including the Siglit) near the mouth of the Mackenzie River had a comparatively varied diet. They hunted caribou, musk-ox, whales, walrus and seal, and, as we have seen, developed large villages. The Copper Inuit lived on Victoria Island and around Coronation Gulf. They used copper found in the area to fashion tools and as an item of trade with neighbouring Inuit. The Iglulik Inuit, who occupied northern Baffin Island and the Melville Peninsula, developed a rich variety of games, customs and arts.

The First Contact

The first Europeans into the Arctic were explorers and whalers. Martin Frobisher reached Baffin Island in 1576. A handful of other Arctic explorers, including Henry Hudson, who sailed into the bay named after him in 1610, followed. British Arctic exploration peaked in the thirty-year period following the end of the Napoleonic Wars in 1815. Suddenly, England found itself with plenty of underutilized ships and unemployed sailors. The search for the Northwest Passage became a major preoccupation.

Edward Parry reached Melville Island in 1819. John Franklin made three trips to the Arctic. In 1819 he reached the Coppermine River by land, returning to explore the area in 1825. Finally in 1845 he set off with two ships, *Erebus* and *Terror*, to navigate the Northwest Passage. The expedition failed and ended in the disappearance of the crews of both ships, touching off a mystery that is still unsolved today. In all, some eight sea and several land expeditions combed the Arctic, first for survivors and later for evidence of Franklin's fate. Recently it was suggested that the crews, caught in the ice, succumbed to lead poisoning from the lead used to seal cans in which their food was stored. Other historians argue that had Franklin (and other explorers) been willing to learn about dress and travel from the Inuit their fate might have been different. When travelling on ice or land the British insisted on having men pull heavy sleighs rather than use dogs. Instead of skins and furs, the explorers insisted on wearing regulation military dress. "Going native" was deemed not acceptable.

The activities of the explorers had little impact on the north and its people. Simply put, they came, they saw and they left.

Close on the heels of the explorers, and in some areas even ahead of them, came the whalers who brought the first major transformations to northern life.

Between 1820 and 1830, about 750 ships visited the Arctic, taking over 8,000 whales. Whalers from Scotland and the

United States were well established in Cumberland Sound at the southeast end of Baffin Island by the 1840s. By the 1890s the industry was based on Herschel Island, just north of the Yukon's Arctic coast. At the height of the whaling activity on that island, it was virtually occupied by the Americans.

The whalers introduced the Inuit to European trade goods. Some whalers wintered over and brought supplies to trade with the Inuit. Trade with the Inuit for furs became more important as the supply of whales decreased and as the demand for whale products dropped. Inuit also began to trade their labour for the whalers' trade goods. Inuit were often hired to help with the whale hunt. In return they received goods such as tea, chewing tobacco, rifles, traps and utensils.

The activities of the whalers are still remembered by many older Inuit. In a December 31, 1987, interview with *The Globe and Mail*, 100-year-old Leah Nutaraq from Iqaluit recalled:

> Their modern equipment was useful to us, so when they didn't come for two summers, we moved to another whaling station ... Whenever I see smoke from the garbage dump, it reminds me of the black smoke that used to tell us a coal-powered whaling ship was coming ... People used to say they could smell the smokestack for days before it appeared.

The community of Igloolik is an example of the effect the whaling trade had on local populations. The Inuit living in that area used to travel inland in the summer to hunt. With the coming of the whalers, they stayed on the coast in the summer so that they could get guns and other goods.

The whalers brought serious disruptions to Inuit life. In the nineteenth century, when the American whaling ships were in port at Herschel Island, a combination of plentiful alcohol and the availability of Inuit women led to unprecedented debauchery. All the Sadlermuit Inuit of Southampton Island in Hudson Bay, who McGhee speculates may have been the last of the Dorset people, died early in the twentieth century from a smallpox epidemic after the Scottish whaling ship, *Active*, visited the island. The last known survivor of the Salliq people of that island died in 1948.

Canada Assumes Responsibility for the North

The BNA Act that created the Dominion of Canada (now known as the Constitution Act, 1867) provided, in section 146, for the admission of new provinces and of "Rupert's Land and the North-Western Territory" into Confederation. Rupert's Land was the land over which Charles II had granted the Hudson's Bay Company (HBC) an exclusive trading licence. It included all lands whose rivers flowed into the Hudson Bay: the prairies, northern Quebec, northern Ontario, the eastern Arctic, and portions of Baffin Island. The North-Western Territory included central and northern Alberta, northwestern Saskatchewan, the Yukon, the central Arctic and all the Mackenzie Valley district. In 1870 the Hudson's Bay Company interest in these lands was transferred to the new Dominion. In acquiring these two territories, Canada was primarily interested in the prairies so that it could fulfil the dream of Confederation, a nation from sea to sea.

Transfer of responsibility for the Arctic islands followed in 1880, when England ceded the islands to Canada by an order-in-council, ostensibly to prevent extension of American jurisdiction into the eastern Arctic. American interests had sought mineral rights on Baffin Island as early as 1874, and both the United States and Norway advanced claims to Queen Elizabeth Island. The transfer made clear that Canadian law was to apply in the Arctic islands.

In practice, Canada was reluctant to assert its jurisdiction, and this may well have been a signal that the Arctic was open territory. The late nineteenth and early twentieth centuries saw much activity in the Arctic, most of it by foreign governments and their nationals, including their whaling fleets. An 1879 meeting of eleven nations at Hamburg, Germany, declared 1882–83 to be the First International Polar Year. Each nation declared that scientific activities would be the focus of its polar activities. As part of the effort the Americans established a research station at Fort Conger on Ellesmere Island (this proved something of a disaster, as only seven of twenty-six men survived the return trip from the station), the British at Fort Rae and the Germans in Cumberland Sound on Baffin Island. Canada established no such station.

Between 1899 and 1903, the Norwegian Otto Sverdrup became the first non-Aboriginal person to visit Axel Heiberg Island, Amund Ringnes Island and Ellef Ringnes Island. From 1903 to 1906 his fellow countryman Roald Amundsen navigated the Northwest Passage. During the same decade, a race was underway to reach the North Pole. The competition was largely dominated by Americans using Canadian territory and the skills of Canadian and Greenlandic Inuit. Americans Robert Peary and Frederick Cook were the main competitors, with Cook claiming to have reached the Pole in 1908 and Peary in 1909. (Questions have been raised as to whether either man actually reached the Pole.)

Also in the early 1900s there were reports that Inuit from Greenland were using Canadian territory—Baffin and Ellesmere islands—as their hunting grounds.

Assertion of Sovereignty

Eventually, such activities prompted the Canadian government to show the flag in the Arctic. While Clifford Sifton, Wilfrid Laurier's Minister of the Interior, is best remembered for his immigration policies, he was also instrumental in establishing a Canadian presence in the Arctic. Captain William Wakeham was dispatched on a reconnaissance mission in 1897 to Hudson Bay and Baffin Island. At a remote whaling station, Kekerton Harbour on Baffin Island, he made a formal declaration of Canadian sovereignty over Baffin and surrounding islands. Six years later, in 1903, Albert P. Low from the Geological Survey office led a mission to Hudson Bay to license any whalers hunting in the bay and the following year he travelled to Ellesmere and Somerset islands where he raised the Canadian ensign and built cairns to symbolize Canada's assertion of sovereignty. A similar mission in 1904 was commanded by Captain Joseph-Elzéar Bernier, who had for a number of years lobbied the federal government to send a Canadian expedition to the North Pole. The government acquired a ship, which was christened the *Arctic*, for Bernier's mission. Between 1909 and 1911, Captain Bernier was given the task of travelling through the Arctic archipelago to show the Canadian flag, and in the words of that voyage's historian, to "take official possession, in the name of Canada, of that great heritage so graciously given to us by England more than 20 years ago, a territory which today is very much prized by foreign nations." In 1909 Bernier unveiled a plaque on Melville Island claiming all the Arctic islands for Canada.

The NWT Act was amended in 1905 to restate Canada's claim to the Arctic islands. In part this action stemmed from an internal government report which indicated that Canada's claim to some of the islands was less than perfect. Two years later, in response to American polar expeditions, New Brunswick Senator Pascal Poirier proposed in the Senate that Canada "make a formal declaration of possession of the land and islands situated in the north of the Dominion, and extending to the North Pole." His proposal gave rise to the sector theory, the idea that each Arctic nation was the owner of a wedge of water and land extending from the eastern and western boundaries of its Arctic coast to the North Pole. The Russian czar and later the Soviet government accepted this theory (which would award them vast territories), but it was rejected by the Americans and Scandinavians. A competing theory being developed at the same time in European circles was the theory of effective occupation to determine sovereignty. Obviously, this theory was not happily received in Canada—it meant that Canada would either have to settle the north or publicly accept the Inuit as full citizens. The latter would have meant a major change in attitudes, for which Canadians were not yet ready.

Between 1913 and 1918 the federal government funded the Canadian Arctic Expedition, co-led by Canadian explorer Vilhjalmur Stefansson. Stefansson was one of the last non-Aboriginal explorers to discover hitherto unknown islands in the Arctic—Brock, Borden and Meighen islands. Then in 1922 the government recommenced the Eastern Arctic Patrol, again under the command of Captain Bernier in the *Arctic*. In addition to showing the Canadian flag, this time the patrol also supplied police posts.

Prompted by rumours that American explorer Donald Mac-Millan was planning to fly over the North Pole, in 1926 the federal government established the Arctic Island Preserve requiring all scientists and explorers to obtain permits before entering the area. At the same time the area was declared off-bounds to all non-Inuit trappers and hunters and the government started to regulate trade in the area. Shipboard trading posts were prohibited as were visits to Inuit camps. Historian Kenneth Coates, in *Canada's Colonies*, suggests that these regulations were inspired by the HBC as a way of keeping independent traders out as much as by any consideration of sovereignty. The preserve was extended again in 1929 and 1942 to include all Arctic islands and a significant portion of the Arctic mainland.

In the 1930s, with a severe economic depression raging and with few challenges to Canada's sovereignty, federal activity in the north was minimal. In 1930 the Canadian government paid the Norwegian Otto Sverdrup $67,000 for his services in exploring the Canadian Arctic, with this payment laying to rest any claim Norway might have to the northern islands. And during the Second Polar Year, 1932–33, Canada established research stations at Coppermine and Chesterfield Inlet. However, the depression forced the government to cut the Arctic patrol in 1932, after its ship the *Arctic* sank. Instead the government contracted with the HBC, at an annual cost of between $23,000 and $27,000, to carry government personnel and supplies. The exercise of Canadian sovereignty at any point was, therefore, dependent upon the length of time the company ship remained there. According to company records, the ship stayed at some posts for less than a day. It was only after World War II that the government again acquired ships for travelling into Arctic waters.

Ironically, Canada ignored one of its strongest claims to sovereignty, the fact that much of the Arctic was occupied by its Inuit people. It would take another fifty years before the government would make that kind of declaration.

The Fur Trade

As the whaling industry faded, the fur trade took over. The HBC began moving north in 1911. At the peak of the Arctic fur trade the company ran over one hundred posts in nearly eighty locations and by 1938, when the fur trade started to decline, it had an absolute monopoly on Arctic trade. By 1923 all Inuit were within travelling distance of a trading post. The Arctic white fox was the staple of the trade.

Historians disagree on the effects of the fur trade. While recognizing that the trade caused significant disruption and harm to Native life, Kenneth Coates argues that it was not nearly as exploitative as suggested by some historians. Coates holds that Aboriginal people were willing participants in the fur trade and influenced its direction, often working for the traders as guides and interpreters. In his view, the Native people wanted European goods and therefore actively sought to trade. Other historians, like Arthur Ray, see the fur trade as the start of welfare dependence for Canada's Native people. Granting them credit forced the Inuit and other Aboriginal people to hunt and trap for products wanted by the traders, to pay off the credit. In particular the market wanted Arctic white fox, an animal not traditionally trapped by the Inuit. Although winter was often the best time for sealing, the winter seal hunt was discontinued by many so as to trap for furs.

The company even made Inuit sign contracts binding hunters to deliver furs to HBC posts for extended periods of time. Richard Diubaldo has uncovered a typical contract used in the 1920s, which read:

I do also hereby agree not to engage in any other employment whatsoever, than that of the said Company, for the said term of five years and to deliver my entire hunt to the said company for the said time of Five years.

In return the hunter was offered the regular price of the furs plus twenty dollars a year.

As on the prairies, the HBC was more than a fur-trading company. In some functions, especially in the delivery of social services, the company came to represent the government. In 1923 the NWT Council issued rules for the issuance of relief. Relief could be issued by a medical officer or the officer in charge of an RCMP detachment, and if neither of those was available then by a designated officer, usually a missionary or trader. Relief was usually in the form of goods obtainable from the trading post. As the depression of the 1930s worsened, the Department of the Interior prescribed that an applicant for a licence to open a trading post had to assume responsibility for destitute Natives. The trading company had to bear the cost of such relief alone unless there was a competing post at the same location.

The fur trade continued the relocation of populations that the whaling trade had begun to some extent. Colin Irwin gives an example of such relocation:

> The Netsilingmiut, who now dominate the population of Chesterfield Inlet, moved there in the 1920s from their traditional hunting ground some 500 miles to the north. Part of the reason for this migration was the opportunity to enter the fur trade with the Hudson's Bay Company which had been established at Chesterfield Inlet in the early 1900s.

On occasion, it was the HBC that moved Inuit to an area so that it could exploit fur resources in that area, though some historians suggest that such moves were encouraged or at least condoned by the government. In 1934 the company moved fifty-two Inuit from various settlements in Baffin Island, particulary Cape Dorset, to Dundas Harbour on Devon Island. Similar company actions brought people to Arctic Bay, Fort Ross and Spence Bay.

The debate over whether these were voluntary or forced moves has been taken up in popular histories. Long-time HBC employee Ernie Lyall wrote in his 1979 biography, *An Arctic Man*:

> So Mr. [Farley] Mowatt made a big thing, a big tragedy about the HBC getting the people to go up to Dundas Harbour and then to Arctic Bay (and later Fort Ross and Spence Bay), trying to show that it was right against the people, that the people didn't want to go, that everything was terrible in Dundas ... And all this just plain wasn't true ... They went to Dundas of their own free will, ... the hunting was good there ...

However willingly or unwillingly the Inuit may have accepted these changes, whaling and the fur trade brought unprecedented disruption to the lives of the people of the north. But in the end it was the government that was to bring the most profound changes of all to Inuit life.

The Government's First Appearance in the North

Until World War II, the question of sovereignty dominated federal concerns about the north. While there were government structures for administering the north, that administration was based in Ottawa and was of the view that as much as possible the Inuit should be allowed to live in their traditional way with minimum government intervention. The provision of social services for the Inuit was largely left to the fur traders and church missionaries.

The 1882 order-in-council that created the administrative districts of Athabaska, Saskatchewan, Alberta and Assiniboia within what was then called the North-West Territories (the territory was later further divided into nine districts, including the Yukon which became a separate territory in 1898) stated that no steps should be taken for the government of the north until there was an influx of population or other circumstances warranting such a government. The Inuit were simply ignored.

In 1905, the provinces of Alberta and Saskatchewan were created from the North-West Territories and an Ottawa-based commissioner was appointed to run the remainder of the territory. The first commissioner was the comptroller of the Royal North-West Mounted Police, assisted by a council who until 1947 were all senior federal bureaucrats. What little administrative service the federal government provided to the north was in the hands of the Department of the Interior, which also handled Indian affairs. Within that department, a special NWT Branch (which later became the NWT and Yukon Branch) was set up after oil was discovered at Norman Wells in the 1920s. During the depression of the 1930s that branch was chopped and the north was placed under the Dominion Lands Branch.

Some years earlier, in 1924, the Indian Act was amended to make the Superintendent of Indian Affairs responsible for Inuit affairs, bringing some 6,538 Inuit under his jurisdiction. The legislation, then as today, made it clear that the Inuit were not Indians under the Indian Act. Responsibility for the Inuit, but not for the Indians of the north, was later transferred to the NWT Commissioner and Council.

Thus by 1930 responsibility for the Inuit was in fact divided among three government departments. The commissioner was nominally the head of government, but actual administration rested with the Department of the Interior, although the Superintendent of Indian Affairs (who also fell under the jurisdiction of the Minister of the Interior) was responsible for Inuit and Indian affairs. In reality, the only government operatives in the Arctic were the RCMP, though a territorial branch of the Interior Department was established in Fort Smith, near the Alberta border, in 1921. In 1936 responsibility for the north was transferred to the Bureau of NWT and Yukon Affairs within the Department of Mines, though Inuit and Indian affairs continued to remain with the Superintendent of Indian Affairs.

The NWMP and British Law Go North

Another major instrument of sovereignty and probably the first contact for many Inuit with the Canadian government was the North-West Mounted Police, the forerunners of the RCMP. In 1903 the government established three posts in the Arctic, the first at Cape Fullerton on the western shore of Hudson Bay and the others at Herschel Island and Fort McPherson, both in the western Arctic. The post at Herschel Island was established not so much to control the social problems on the island as to show the Canadian flag among the American whalers.

Other police posts were established for the same reason. Speaking to the House of Commons Committee of Supply in 1922, Lomer Gouin, Justice Minister and Attorney-General, justified the $60,000 needed to create three additional police posts in the Arctic islands: "It is necessary to protect our rights against foreigners; to protect our fisheries, and to take care of our property generally." Posts were also established at Dundas Harbour on Devon Island, and at Bache Peninsula on Ellesmere Island. There were no permanent residents at either location. By the 1920s the RCMP had adopted a policy of establishing a police post at every location where there was a trading post.

While the need to assert Canada's sovereignty was a strong motivation for sending the police north, a series of murders of whites in the 1910s and early 1920s raised a cry in southern Canada that the Inuit be taught British justice.

In the fall of 1913 two Catholic priests, Fathers La Roux and Rouvière, went missing after working with the Copper Inuit. Following a dispute over a rifle, an Inuit elder advised the priests to leave camp. Two other Inuit followed them—their version was that they were travelling to meet family, the prosecution's theory was that they planned to murder the priests. The two Inuit, Sinnisiak and Uluksuk, testified that the priests threatened them and forced them to pull their sleds. As the priests were armed the Inuit believed their lives might be in danger, and so they killed the priests in self-defence.

Shortly after the disappearance of the priests, church officials called in the RNWMP. In a three-year land expedition covering more than ten thousand kilometres, the RNWMP succeeded in tracking down the two accused. They brought them, and all the witnesses and interpreters, to Edmonton for trial. As they were the first Inuit to be tried under Canadian law, their trials gained international attention.

Sinnisiak was tried first. The prosecutor, Charles McCaul, made clear that this was more than a murder trial. In a departure from the usual, McCaul's morning-long opening address to the jury amounted to a harangue on the importance of British justice asserting itself in the north, rather than an overview of the Crown's case.

> I have said this is an important trial.... These remote savages, really cannibals, the Eskimo of the Arctic have got to be taught to recognize the authority of the British Crown ... For the first time in history these people, these Arctic people ... will be brought in contact with and taught what is the white man's justice.

McCaul went on to point out that if "the white man's justice" was not instilled in the Inuit, no white man could safely travel the north.

Later, in his closing remarks, James Wallbridge, the defence lawyer, summed up his case in the following words:

> Sinnisiak sits in his box, he sees with his eyes what is taking place, but he does not comprehend. He can not understand what we are doing. It is a great question whether a man of a stone age tribe, a man who hunts for

daily food, can in common justice have his deeds judged by the standards of modern civilization. The Magna Carta said a man was entitled to have a trial by his peers. Is it possible to have this man judged by his peers?

Sinnisiak was acquitted. But neither the prosecutor nor the judge, Horace Harvey, were happy with this result. They believed that sympathetic portrayals of the two Inuit in the local papers had influenced the jury.

A new trial was held in Calgary, in which both accused were convicted. They were spared the death sentence, however, and in fact ended up working as special constables for the RNWMP several years later.

Another case, this time in the eastern Arctic, appears to illustrate conflicting Inuit and white approaches to justice and community preservation. The RCMP were sent to Pond Inlet at the north end of Baffin Island in 1921 to investigate the murder of a private trader, Robert Janes, the year before. Apparently, he had threatened to shoot dogs belonging to several Inuit hunters. The Inuit, fearing that the loss of their dogs might mean eventual starvation, decided the man was a threat to the community and had to be eliminated. Three Inuit were charged and tried before a jury composed of the crew from the Eastern Arctic Patrol. One was acquitted, one found guilty of aiding and abetting and the third was found guilty of manslaughter.

The RCMP and its predecessor the RNWMP went north to serve as a symbol of Canadian sovereignty and bring "white man's justice" to its people. Once there, they found themselves playing a number of more prosaic roles as well. They were census takers, postmasters, welfare officers and administrators of government policy, but their most important role was to show the flag to foreigners and Inuit alike.

Education and Health

Education and health services were left to the religious missions, who sometimes received government compensation for their efforts. By 1943 there were eleven hospitals in the NWT, nine run by missionaries and two by mining companies. Only two of those hospitals, at Chesterfield and Pangnirtung, were in the eastern Arctic.

Mission schools were devoted to Christian education. And while initially reluctant to fund such education, by 1931 the federal government had relented and was providing nearly $13,000 for eight mission schools in the north. Yet the churches had doubts as to how much effort should be devoted to Inuit education, even though they were responsible for the introduction of a written form of Inuktitut. So did the government. In 1934 a government official wrote that the Inuit of the NWT "are not yet sufficiently advanced for the 'white man's system of education.'" There was only one school in the eastern Arctic, at Pangnirtung on Baffin Island. Canada ignored the successes that the Danish were having with Inuit education in Greenland, and the Americans were having in Alaska. Keith Crowe, in *A History of the Aboriginal People*, documents Canada's priorities: In 1939 the federal government was spending twelve dollars per Inuit on education, health and welfare; in Alaska the figure was thirteen dollars and in Greenland it was forty-four. But Canadian expenditures on police services amounted to seventeen dollars per Inuit while Alaska spent forty-one cents and Greenland spent nothing.

Things began to change during World War II. The start of the war saw the need for more government planning and intervention in the economy. This brought an influx of new civil servants to Ottawa, many of them university professors and scholars who believed that governments had a responsibility to relieve human suffering and poverty. At the same time the need to defend the north and its role as an air route to Europe meant that government officials became conscious of the north and the Inuit fact.

The war brought the military, particularly Americans, to the north, along with journalists. Even before the United States formally declared war in December 1941, they had built air bases at Churchill, Coral Harbour on Southampton Island, Frobisher Bay and Fort Chimo (now known as Kuujjuaq) in Quebec. Once they entered the war, their activities in Canada's Arctic increased significantly. At the height of the war the Americans were running two routes to ferry planes and supplies to the war in Europe—a northwestern route starting in Edmonton and an eastern route using Frobisher Bay. Estimates are that some 43,000 Americans, probably three times Canada's northern population, were working on northern defence projects in 1943. They, in turn, were able to observe the plight of the Inuit. American medical officers attached to the military publicly commented on the poor health of the Inuit. Ottawa's response was to call in the U.S. military attaché and complain that these criticisms amounted to a breach of protocol.

The Inuit's destitution resulted in part from the collapse of the fur trade in the 1930s. The value of a white fox pelt dropped from forty dollars to near ten dollars. Starvation became commonplace. The need to deal with this situation would eventually bring about a major change in the Inuit's relationship with the federal government: Canada's estimated 7,700 Inuit became wards of the state. As a first step, starting in 1941 the government began a policy of giving Inuit numbers so as to keep track of them. According to Ernie Lyall,

Eskimos were given numbers because they generally only had one name and a lot of Eskimos had the same ones, and sometimes they even changed their name to something different. All this was very confusing in the records that people were trying to keep, like the RCMP, missionaries, doctors, even the Bay in some places. So the government decided to give them numbers, which I think was a good thing.

They were encouraged—some say they were forced—to move into settlements. It was in the period following World War II that the modern north was born.

3

The Modern North

Much has happened in the eastern Arctic since World War II. Government settlements were established for the Inuit—ostensibly to make it easier to deliver social services to them. At the same time national interests began to dominate the north: the need to exploit resources on a large scale, and, once again, the need to assert Canadian sovereignty. Then, starting in the 1960s, Ottawa loosened some of its grip on the Northwest Territories and began to transfer power to the territorial government to the point where today that government has nearly the same powers as a province.

The Inuit had little say in these developments in spite of the impact they had on their lives. The idea of settlements and the social service scheme that came with it were devised in Ottawa and assumed to be in their best interests. As the north was opened up for resource development in the late 1950s the Inuit saw their land and way of life threatened, but no one asked them about their concerns. The Inuit knew the eastern Arctic better than anyone, yet it was only in the late 1980s that Canada even began to consider that their occupancy and use of these lands might be its best claim to sovereignty over disputed passages in the Arctic. And as for the transfer of power from Ottawa to Yellowknife, as far as the Inuit were concerned the transfer was to a foreign government, for they did not see—and still do not see—the GNWT as their government.

These themes have shaped the modern north and led the Inuit to conclude that someday they must have their own government. More important, the Inuit believe that some of the federal government's unilateral actions have left them in a dependent state and that only when they are masters of their own territory will they be masters of their own lives.

The Growth of Settlements

The 1940s, 50s and 60s saw the growth of settlements where but a few years earlier there was only a trading post, a police station and perhaps a religious mission. In other instances communities developed around military installations and newly established administrative centres. Not always was this relocation voluntary.

For example, Inuvik, begun in the late fifties, was chosen to be the administrative centre for the western Arctic and a replacement for the Aboriginal community of Aklavik, which federal officials believed would wash away into the Mackenzie River. (It continues to exist to this day.) Even though the Indian and Inuit people of Aklavik refused to abandon their homes, Inuvik's future was assured when the oil and gas boom spread into the western Arctic. Similarly, the Diefenbaker government chose Frobisher Bay, now Iqaluit, as the administrative centre for the eastern Arctic. It had started out as a U.S. Air Force base in World War II. Resolute Bay started as an RCAF base and service point for radar and weather stations in the high Arctic. When a ship carrying supplies for the building of a major service point became icebound at the site, the town was built right there. In the early and mid-1950s, Inuit were moved there to provide a local supply of labour.

So too, when Canada and the United States built the Distant Early Warning (DEW) line across the Arctic between 1954 and 1957, many of the more than twenty sites attracted Inuit seeking jobs and social services. Some of those sites, such as Cambridge Bay (Ikaluktutiak), became regional administrative centres. Ironically, the U.S.-Canada agreement dealing with construction of the line provided that the Inuit lifestyle should not be disturbed.

Canada's assertion of sovereignty over remote areas of the north also led to the establishment of new Inuit communities. The most famous and controversial case was the relocation of some eleven families from Port Harrison (now Inukjuak), in northern Quebec, to Grise Fiord on Ellesmere Island in 1953. The transfer meant a serious adjustment for the Inuit. In Quebec they had hunted ducks and other birds; on Ellesmere Island they had to rely on sea mammals and polar bear. Summer in northern Quebec lasted three and a half months; on Ellesmere Island it lasted six weeks, and winter there was sunless.

Although the federal government maintained that the Inuit were voluntarily relocated because of an impending food shortage and the fear that they would become welfare dependents, in 1989 it agreed to spend nearly $250,000 to cover the moving costs of Inuit who wanted to return to northern Quebec. But that did not end the matter. Inuit leaders had been pressing for a $10 million heritage fund as compensation. Allegations were made that Inuit in the high Arctic were treated like slaves and that Inuit women were sexually assaulted by the police. "Only after the women were used for sex purposes would they [the RCMP] give us food," Martha Flaherty testified before the House of Commons Aboriginal Affairs Committee. This was disputed by others, including a retired RCMP officer who had served at Grise Fiord in the late 1950s.

The government position that the relocation was voluntary was supported by the Inuit translator who worked for the government during the move. But in its June 1990 report, the Aboriginal Affairs Committee concluded that Inuit had been relocated to Grise Fiord and Resolute Bay to demonstrate Canada's sovereignty there. Among other things, the committee called for a federal apology to the Inuit, public recognition of the role they played in asserting Canadian sovereignty and compensation for the wrongdoing the Inuit had suffered.

Instead of following the committee's recommendations, Thomas Siddon, the federal Minister of Indian Affairs, hired an independent consultant, which concluded that "the main reason for the decision by the Government to encourage some Inuit families to relocate to the High Arctic ... was a concern to improve the living conditions of the Inuit." Siddon announced that the government was not prepared to pay further compensation.

However, following a Canadian Human Rights Commission report released in January 1992 which agreed substantially with the Aboriginal Affairs Committee (but did not address the issue of compensation), in a surprise move Ottawa announced that it was willing to apologize and talk to the Inuit about their demands.

Of course, in some cases Inuit did move voluntarily. Schools and health centres were being established in the communities, so for Inuit wanting such services a move to the community made sense. Less than three years after a 1948 government study had recommended the establishment of day schools, nine such schools were established throughout Inuit country. According to Richard Diubaldo, by 1951, of 8,646 Inuit, nearly 900 were attending schools, of whom some 300 were at federal schools and the balance at missionary schools. And in the 1960s the federal government made a decision to build a nursing station in every Inuit community.

By this time, the government was concerned with presenting the benefits for the Inuit of settling in communities. A 1972 Indian and Northern Affairs report entitled *Eskimo Housing As Planned Culture Change* argued that a scattered population is difficult to administer, and there is less likelihood of starvation if everyone is in a settlement (and less likelihood of criticism by the press). When the people live in settlements it is easier to establish health stations; it is easier to distribute welfare payments.

Unfortunately, the attempt to build instant communities often left much to be desired. The 1972 government report detailed some of the problems that resulted:

> Crash programs were undertaken without a clear concept of the role the government wished to assume and what role the government wished Eskimos to assume. The government has created a need on the part of the Eskimo for many material items and services associated with new housing, and contributed to the acceptance of many Euro-Canadian values and ideas ... They were encouraged to buy their own homes, then encouraged to rent them ... They are told they must be educated to perform jobs which are their new and further form of subsistence, but then are largely denied jobs other than those in menial capacities. They are told that they must assume responsibility but are not given adequate opportunity to do so.

With the growth of settlements came a significant number of federal civil servants to administer education, health, welfare and economic development. This movement of civil servants created a class society. In his book, *The People's Land*, Hugh Brody argued that the federal employees lived a southern middle-class lifestyle at government expense while local Inuit lived a subsistence welfare standard.

It rapidly became obvious that moving Inuit (whether voluntarily or otherwise) to settlements was creating as many problems as it was solving. Population increased rapidly—average family size increased from two children in pre-settlement days to families of between six and ten children—but employment opportunities were virtually non-existent in most communities. These problems, arising from the rapid transformation of Inuit society, are the ones the Inuit hope will be effectively addressed by the creation of Nunavut.

Social Conditions Among the Inuit

In a 1964 technical report for the Arctic Institute of North America, noted anthropologist Diamond Jenness remarked:

> But why should we confine our Eskimos to the Arctic? If nature now denies them a livelihood in their ancient homeland, why should they not migrate elsewhere ... They may disappear as a separate people ... but surely it is preferable that they should succumb struggling for a better life in southern Canada than rotting away in the Arctic on government doles.... We should bring them in family groups, settle them in small colonies ...

Inuit were indeed moved south in large numbers in the 1950s, not as part of any relocation scheme but rather to combat a major tuberculosis epidemic. The first public discussion of the idea of relocation appears to have surfaced in 1957 with the House of Commons Eskimo Affairs Committee. It involved resettling released tubercular patients at an abandoned hospital site near Selkirk, Manitoba. Today evidence shows that even before World War II there was reason to be concerned about tuberculosis. Dr. Keith Rogers reported in a 1938 health survey that there were no facilities in the north for doing X-rays among the Inuit and no way of checking for tuberculosis. But the government's *Canadian Resources Bulletin* for 1938 reported that the rate of tuberculosis among Inuit was less than among southerners. In spite of such government assurances, during the early 1940s the tuberculosis rate among the Inuit reached 1,100 per 100,000 persons, compared to 50 per 100,000 for Canada as a whole. Epidemics of meningitis, respiratory diseases and other diseases were also common.

Once the federal government accepted that there was a tuberculosis crisis among the Inuit—after prodding from American military doctors—the battle was fought by transporting nearly 20 percent of the Inuit population thousands of kilometres south in circumstances more reminiscent of the roundup of labour for concentration camps than humane health care. The annual Arctic patrol carried out shipboard X-rays starting in 1947. If tuberculosis was suspected the patient was required to remain aboard ship, for fear that if allowed off the ship, the patient wouldn't return. The patients were taken to sanatoria in Toronto, Montreal, Hamilton and Edmonton. No effort was made to inform family members of the progress or whereabouts of their kin in the south. At the end of treatment patients were loaded on a plane or ship and dropped off at various settlements, not always the ones where they had originated.

In a *Northern Review* article, historian P. Gerry Nixon estimated that between 1953 and 1964 some 3,700 Inuit from the NWT were hospitalized in southern institutions for an average stay of 28 months. A 1962 government memo put the number of Inuit currently in southern hospitals at over 1,600.

The plight of the Inuit was compounded by the continuing collapse of the fur trade in the 1940s. By the end of the decade white fox pelts were selling for less than five dollars, compared to nearly twenty dollars a few years earlier. People who had become dependent on the trade suddenly found that they were reduced to starvation. Government support programs replaced the fur trade as the main source of income in the north. The way in which that support was handed out is indicative of how the government viewed the Inuit. After family allowances were introduced in 1945 the Inuit received their allowances in kind after applying to the local police or trading post, where accounts were apparently often handled in a perfunctory way. Only items on a list sent to all trading posts could be acquired, including pablum, Eskimo cereal, dried or evaporated milk, dry powdered eggs, canned fruits, juices and vegetables and vitamin B flour. It was only in 1960 that the government starting giving cheques to the Inuit themselves.

Combined with the move to settlements, the collapse of the fur trapping economy and the consequent dependence on government assistance may have laid the basis for a series of persistent social problems in the eastern Arctic. Colin Irwin, in his controversial 1988 study *Lords of the Arctic: Wards of the State*, states the following conclusion: "Most of the Inuit living in the Arctic in the year 2025 will probably be second generation wards of the state living out their lives in "Arctic Ghettos" plagued by increasing rates of crime ..." While Irwin's report was criticized on many grounds, no one has denied that he has pointed out some of the major problems facing the north. It is predictions like his that have given the Inuit the incentive to take their future into their own hands with the creation of Nunavut.

A major problem has been the high attrition rate of Inuit from the education system. Only 34 percent of Inuit schoolchildren reach grade 9 as compared to 80 percent of the population nationally. A mere 15 percent of Inuit graduate from high school as compared to 52 percent of all Canadians. Fewer than 1 percent of Inuit students attend university.

Why do community-based schools, especially those in the more remote communities, have such a poor success rate? the committee preparing the 1989 *Scone Report: Building Our Economic Future* asked. The committee's conclusion was this:

> One of the most significant factors is the lack of a viable economic base in the local community. If students cannot see the results of education, if they cannot link their education to a job and a viable paycheque, there is little incentive to pursue an education.... Families that were once able to live fairly independent lifestyles have now become highly dependent upon the government welfare cheque. The lack of work and dependence upon welfare has had a widespread negative impact upon native peoples, their social lives, and their institutions ...

In a *Globe and Mail* interview, Liz Rose, an Inuk living in Iqaluit, said, "We've raised this false expectation that when they finish grade 12, they will have a job. But there are so few jobs."

In fact, rates of unemployment for the Arctic are variously estimated at 12 percent in official reports and as high as 72 percent by some social scientists. The low figure is from Statistics Canada and only counts those persons actively looking for a job. But in small communities where everyone knows when there is a job available and there are few openings, the government figure distorts the true picture.

In its report, *Unfinished Business: An Agenda for all Canadians in the 1990s*, the House of Commons Standing Committee on Aboriginal Affairs reported that 40 percent of Inuit were employed as compared to 60 percent of all Canadians.

Even traditional hunting pursuits are difficult to maintain. To outfit oneself for hunting will probably require several thousand dollars. Snowmobile prices start at four thousand dollars. Add to that fuel at well over a dollar a litre. Very quickly, one can see that a significant investment is required to go out on the land to hunt and trap. Colin Irwin has concluded that an active year-round hunt costs about ten thousand dollars a year. In short, most people probably need employment income to support their hunting and trapping activities. To add to the complicated equation Inuit, like other Aboriginal people, have faced an attempt by European nations to ban the trade in furs. As a result, the demand for furs has dropped significantly. In 1980–81, there were 37,000 white fox pelts harvested; by the 1988–89 the number had fallen to 1,900, producing an income of $24,000 territory-wide.

The depressed fur market is reflective of the economy in general. The *Scone Report* painted a bleak picture of northern communities and their economic prospects. The report classified only seven communities in the NWT as "developed," meaning that they have good transportation links, are either administrative or resource centres and have a significant private sector. Only one of those—Nanisivik, a mining town—was in the eastern Arctic, and unlike most other eastern Arctic communities the majority of its population is non-Native. Six communities were deemed to be "swing communities," having high unemployment but market potential. Five of these are in the eastern Arctic: Iqaluit, Pangnirtung, Baker Lake, Arviat and Rankin Inlet. Forty-six communities were classified as "underdeveloped"; their population was mostly Native, education levels were below grade 9 and official unemployment rates ran at 27 percent. Those communities made up 57.7 percent of the territorial population; because of their relatively high birth rate the report estimated that they would make up 62.5 percent of the NWT population by the year 2001. Because of the increasing birth rate, simply to maintain the current low level of employment in those communities would require the creation of an additional 2,789 jobs, the report concluded.

The birth rate in the eastern Arctic is estimated at 4 percent per annum, one of the highest in the world. This rate means a doubling of the population every eighteen years. The percentage of Inuit who are below fourteen years of age is almost twice that of the rest of Canada. By the turn of the century the Inuit population is expected to exceed 40,000.

The population growth in turn is giving rise to a serious housing shortage. *Arctic* magazine, in its July/August 1990 issue, put it this way: the north needs 3,000 new housing units, but the NWT Housing Corporation can only afford to supply 300 units a year at a time when new households are being formed at the rate of 150 a year.

Poor housing, poverty and underdevelopment take a deadly toll. The Commons Aboriginal Affairs Committee reports that infant deaths for Inuit are 28 per thousand as compared to 8 per thousand for all Canadians. The life expectancy of Canadians is from eight to fifteen years higher than that of the Inuit of the NWT.

Nor are the prospects for economic self-sufficiency in the eastern Arctic good in the near future. In early 1992 there was only one operating mine, the one at Nanisivik. While there was some petroleum activity in the high Arctic (in the westernmost region of the proposed Nunavut), experts seem to agree that oil prices will have to rise substantially to make production of that oil economical. So besides government, the only significant industry is tourism. And while the industry is growing, its impact on the NWT is still marginal. The *Scone Report* estimated that tourism produced $25 million of revenue out of a total GDP of $2 billion, nearly all of it concentrated in the Fort Smith–Yellowknife corridor. Thus for Nunavut to become reality either its residents will have to accept short-term cuts in services or the federal government will have to put in additional money.

Some ideas have been floated as possible solutions. Colin Irwin argues that anyone who is not retired and does not have a job be given minimum wage. That person would then have three alternatives: to work at some form of community service (working at a daycare, teaching traditional crafts or hunting skills, collecting oral histories, helping clean up the town or helping construct housing and community facilities); to support himself or herself at school; or to use the subsidy as a hunting and fishing support program. He estimates that such a program would cost about $30 million for Nunavut, not including the savings that would be achieved from reduction in welfare and unemployment insurance costs. This cost is less than 3.75 percent of the annual budget of the GNWT.

Some of his ideas might yet be implemented. As part of the 1990 agreement-in-principle on land claims the parties agreed to study the feasibility of a wildlife harvesting income support program.

Other scenarios have been proposed to improve the well-being of the people of the eastern Arctic. One suggestion has been that the Inuit should be given a greater role in Arctic search and rescue and in defending Canadian sovereignty. (Several hundred Inuit already serve in the Canadian Rangers—a part-time militia unit whose duty is to report unusual foreign military activity.) In April 1990, in a speech reminiscent of John Diefenbaker's northern vision, Gordon Wray, then territorial Minister of Economic Development and Tourism, floated the idea of a highway to the Keewatin joining Baker Lake, Rankin Inlet, Chesterfield Inlet, Whale Cove and Arviat to either Churchill or Yellowknife. "Transportation is the key to the entire economic future," he said in a *News/North* interview. Several months later, in the fall of 1990, the GNWT released a new transportation strategy that called for a major road construction program which would add 4,800 kilometres of highway over a period of twenty years, including nearly 3,000 kilometres in the Keewatin and Kitikmeot regions.

These are but ideas. They are a long way from becoming economic reality. In the meantime, the socio-economic circumstances remain bleak for the eastern Arctic.

The Challenge of Resource Development

Since the early 1960s Canada's northern agenda has been driven not only by the need to address Inuit social welfare problems, but also by the prospect of resource development and the need to assert Canada's sovereignty in the north. Canada's northern Aboriginal people see resource development as a major threat to their land and their way of life. It was this that propelled many of them to press for settlement of their land claims.

In his 1958 election campaign, John Diefenbaker promised major development in the north, including a six-year, $100 million plan to build roads to Canada's northern mineral resources. With government encouragement, oil exploration on Sabine Peninsula, Melville Island began in 1959 and the first well in Canada's high Arctic was drilled there in 1961. Exploration in the Beaufort Sea–Mackenzie Delta began in late 1960s, with the first oil well drilled in 1973. By 1971 exploration permits had been granted to more than 75 million hectares of Arctic Canada.

In 1969, Panarctic Oils, a consortium formed in 1967 in which the Canadian government had a 45 percent interest, discovered gas at Drake Point on Melville Island. Nearly a decade later, in 1978, the company announced that it had "completed the world's first offshore gas well on the sea bottom below the ice of the Arctic Ocean .... in the Drake Point field." Dome Petroleum, which had been active in the Arctic since the early 1960s, quickly became a leader in offshore drilling with drilling ships and platforms designed for Arctic service. It received its initial exploration permits in the 1960s and in 1973 applied for permission to drill in the Beaufort Sea. The federal cabinet granted permission without consulting local Inuit who used the area for hunting and fishing. After protests by environmentalists and Aboriginal groups who produced evidence that a well blowout in the Beaufort Sea could be one of the world's worst environmental disasters, cabinet reconsidered. Permission was finally granted in 1976.

In the late 1970s the federal government developed the National Energy Program (NEP) to assure Canadian self-sufficiency in oil and gas and to ensure that the industry remained in Canadian hands. Incentives (up to 80 percent of the cost) for drilling new wells in frontier areas was offered to Canadian companies. At the same time the federal government reserved a 25 percent share of any new oil and gas finds to itself. As the federal government could not legislate resource development within provincial boundaries, the north was one of the main areas where the program applied. (When the Conservative government came to power in 1984 many aspects of the NEP program that pertained to the north were abolished.)

These resource development decisions were made in the so-called national interest, with little attention paid to the concerns of local Inuit people. As Peter Cumming wrote in the early 1980s, "The history of northern development in Canada demonstrates how government has paid lip-service to native peoples' and environmentalists' concerns, while all the time pressing relentlessly forward for resource development."

Things began to change somewhat in 1984. In that year, the Amauligak structure in the Beaufort Sea was discovered, with an estimated 700 to 800 million barrels of oil. At the same time Esso Resources discovered a major gas field just south of Tuktoyaktuk. The discovery of oil and gas in the Mackenzie Delta–Beaufort Sea area prompted the government to settle the land claim of the Inuvialuit (the western Arctic Inuit). By this 1984 agreement (the preliminary agreement had been signed in 1978) the federal government gave a substantial land interest to the Inuvialuit and set up structures that allow for Inuvialuit input into resource development. The agreement was an important precedent. It established that the Aboriginal interest was as important as exploitation of resources.

On the heels of this exploration activity have come the announcements of various schemes designed to get the oil and gas south. The Mackenzie Valley Pipeline was halted after the Berger Inquiry, headed by B.C. Supreme Court judge Thomas Berger, recommended a ten-year halt to further development in order that Native claims, including those of the Inuvialuit, could be settled. A similar scheme to build a pipeline along the Alaska Highway came to a halt after an inquiry led by the UBC law dean, Kenneth Lysyk, recommended a freeze on development for a minimum of four years so that Aboriginal concerns could be addressed.

The Arctic Pilot Project, backed by Crown-owned Petro-Canada, involved a plan to liquefy natural gas and ship it south through Lancaster Sound in two specially constructed ice-breaking tankers, each some three hundred metres long and capable of travelling through ice as thick as two metres. When the $1.5 billion scheme was publicly unveiled in 1979 one of the first opponents was the Inuit Tapirisat of Canada, who called on the federal government to block it until the Inuit land claim was settled. Many Greenlanders also opposed the project.

A competing project, the $6–to–$10 billion Polar Gas Project, involved shipping gas by pipeline from the high Arctic to southern Canada along a route following the shores of the Hudson Bay. This scheme would have involved putting pipelines across some 270 kilometres of open channels between Arctic islands. A branch line to bring Mackenzie Delta gas was also envisaged. This scheme, too, faced opposition from the Inuit.

As the price of oil and gas dropped in the early 1980s most of the plans to transport northern oil and gas were put on hold. But after several years of dormancy new schemes began to emerge. In 1985 Panarctic Oils a sent a trial shipload of oil from its Arctic base to Montreal; in 1990 it announced plans for submarine tankers. A new pipeline has now been proposed by a consortium of Esso Resources, Shell and Gulf Canada to bring gas south from the Mackenzie Delta–Beaufort Sea area. Two routes have been discussed, one along the Mackenzie River and the other following the Dempster Highway. As a first step, in 1989 the National Energy Board gave the consortium a conditional licence (subject to cabinet approval and other conditions) to export 260 billion cubic metres of gas over a twenty-year period starting no sooner than 1996.

Resource development has once again heightened Canada's sovereignty concerns in the north. At issue is whether oil can be shipped through the Northwest Passage without Canadian consent. The United States maintains that the passage is an international strait and therefore open to international shipping.

The passage, incidentally, is not one single waterway, as its name might imply. There are in fact dozens of possible routes through the Arctic islands, but only two that are practical for shipping. Both involve sailing between Baffin Island and Greenland into Lancaster Sound, at which point they diverge, one leading northward and the other, suitable to ships of shallower draft, southward along the mainland coastline. No matter which route is followed, a significant portion falls into the 3.8 million square kilometres of land traditionally used by the Inuit. The 1976 Inuit Land Use and Occupancy Project showed that Lancaster Sound and all of the southern route along the mainland coastline fall within seas traditionally used by the Inuit.

In 1968, the year that huge oil discoveries were made in the Prudhoe Bay area on the north coast of Alaska, the U.S. Coast Guard informed Canada that it would be sending an ice-breaker to accompany the tanker *Manhattan* through the Northwest Passage. Canadian permission for the voyage was not sought, though Canada did have observers on board and provided an ice-breaker of its own.

Prime Minister Pierre Trudeau responded by proclaiming Canadian sovereignty over all Arctic islands and offshore resources. Then in the early 1970s his government passed the Arctic Waters Pollution Prevention Act, which gave Canada the authority to control pollution in a hundred-mile zone—an indirect attempt to assert sovereignty over the Northwest passage without doing so overtly.

In early 1988 Canada and the United States signed an agreement by which the United States would seek Canadian consent before sailing through the Northwest Passage. Still, the Americans did not accept Canada's contention that the waters between the Arctic islands are Canadian territory.

Beginning in the 1950s, Canadian courts have found that they have criminal jurisdiction over Inuit in the waters of the Northwest Passage. Yet only in the mid-1980s did the federal government begin to acknowledge that the Inuit were important players in the sovereignty fight in their own right. In its June 1986 report a Special Joint Committee of the Senate and Commons on Canada's International Relations concluded: "The Inuit are Canada's most important support in the Arctic and the government's policy should reflect this perception."

This position was further reinforced in the 1990 agreement-in-principle signed by the federal government and the Inuit of the eastern Arctic. That agreement recognizes the principle that "Canada's sovereignty over the waters of the arctic archipelago is supported by Inuit use and occupancy."

Self-Government in the North

As the process of settlement was completed and in the midst of the northern oil and gas boom, Ottawa decided to turn over some of its powers to the territorial government. In 1967 the Carrothers commission on the development of the NWT government, whose work is discussed in more detail in the next chapter, recommended transfer of specific powers to the territorial government and that the administrative capital of the territories be moved to Yellowknife—which had become the largest community thanks to gold mining—from Fort Smith. For the most part the federal government accepted the commission's recommendations. In 1969 the federal government transferred responsibility for education, welfare, economic development and municipal affairs to the territorial government.

Initially, the territorial government was not an elected one and for the most part it represented the small business interests of the western NWT. Since 1905 the head of government of the NWT has been the commissioner, appointed by Ottawa, originally assisted by a nine-member appointed council. In 1951, for the first time, three council members were elected, representing electoral districts in the western NWT. A fourth elected position was added in 1954, also to represent a western seat. The first elected representation for the eastern Arctic came in 1966 when three elected seats were added, to represent the eastern Arctic, the central Arctic, and the Keewatin. By the time power was transferred to the NWT in 1967, only five members of the twelve-member council were appointees. By 1975 all fifteen members of the council were elected, and shortly after, it adopted the name Legislative Assembly. By 1992, the number of seats stood at twenty-four. The commissioner's role changed too, from virtually running the government to playing a role similar to that of a provincial lieutenant-governor.

In a departure from the practice in southern legislatures and even that in neighbouring Yukon, partisan politics did not become a feature of the NWT Assembly. Decisions, for the most part, are reached by consensus, and the government leader is chosen by the entire Assembly.

Early in 1990, the Legislative Assembly announced that a permanent Assembly building would be built for the first time. A public bond subscription was held to raise money for the building, and the site was formally dedicated on June 27, 1991. Ironically, plans to build a home for the Assembly were being developed at the same time as the process was underway to divide the Territory.

After the 1969 transfer of power, one of the first pieces of legislation passed by the territorial council was an ordinance allowing communities to declare themselves hamlets, even if they had no tax base. Until communities reached hamlet status they were managed by an appointed settlement manager, who had the option of taking advice from a local advisory council. (The first Inuit advisory council had been established in 1957 at Baker Lake with the purpose of providing a forum for discussing local issues and informing local police, nurses, teachers and northern service officers of their views.)

Today, the territorial government has assumed many of the same powers that southern provinces have. Jurisdiction over prosecutions in criminal matters, control over local airports, roads and highways, and control over labour legislation have been discussed for transfer. Crown lands—which include most of the land—remain in federal hands, as do mineral and petroleum production. In 1988 the federal and NWT governments had signed an agreement-in-principle calling for the "phased transfer to the Government of the Northwest Territories of the administrative and legislative powers to manage oil and gas resources." Shortly afterwards, negotiations on the transfer reached a stalemate awaiting further talks on the Dene/Métis land claims, which had broken down.

There is, however, a major difference between powers exercised by the territorial government and a province. Provinces exercise powers under section 92 of the Constitution Act, 1867, which sets out their powers. Territorial powers, however, are exercised under federal legislation: the Northwest Territories Act enumerates the powers of the territorial council and allows the federal government by order-in-council to transfer further powers to the GNWT—and like any federal legislation, it can be amended at any time by unilateral action.

There are also some major differences in the operation of the territorial government. A practice developed of holding regional meetings between settlement leaders and the Yellowknife government. Out of this, participants realized the importance of speaking in a common regional voice to the central government. As a result, this practice was formalized and the Baffin Regional Council was formed in 1977 and formally established by legislation in 1980. Territorial legislation passed in 1983 led to the development of other councils; those in Nunavut include the Kitikmeot and Keewatin regional councils in addition to the one in Baffin. The concept of such councils was that they would co-ordinate all government activities in their region.

Officially, the policy of the territorial government has been to decentralize. In its 1991 position paper on political and constitutional development, the NWT executive council stressed that one of the main elements of northern constitutional development was "the continuation of the transfer of responsibility to the community level of government, and the realization of aboriginal self government in the context of public government at the community and territorial level."

Government in the north is expensive; for the most part, that expense is covered by the federal treasury. Nearly 80 percent of the GNWT's $1 billion dollar plus budget comes from Ottawa. The largest expenditure is for education, followed by public works and highways, health, social services and housing. According to a 1988 discussion paper on political and constitutional development released by the NWT government, expenditures per person in the Territory were three times what they were in the south. The paper further reported that only 18 percent of the NWT government's revenue was derived from the north.

That information was confirmed by the 1989 *Scone Report*, which reported that the largest source of gross domestic product was public administration, accounting for 28 percent of the estimated $2 billion dollar GDP. Put another way, the report found that 9 out of every 20 employees in the NWT worked for the government, whereas in the rest of Canada it was 4 out of 20. After the Yukon, the NWT, with a ratio of one public servant for every 8.7 people, has the highest ratio of civil servants of any Canadian jurisdiction. In the NWT, 46 percent of employment wages came from government, as opposed to 21 percent in Canada as a whole.

By the 1980s the territorial government had become almost too large. The 1988 paper *Directions for the 1990s* complained:

Our government is unique in that it is based on consensus decision-making and public participation and consult-

ation. That has led to the creation of many special purpose committees, societies and boards at the community
level, in addition to and often independent of elected
municipal and community governments. These bodies
have reduced the effectiveness and control of elected
community councils, placed overwhelming burdens on
individual community leaders, and made the process of
governing the NWT more difficult and less efficient. The
addition of a variety of regional boards and bodies further
complicates this already complex government system.

A 1988 discussion paper on political and constitutional
development in the NWT pointed out that the Territories supported 1,500 elected politicians. At the same time there were
800 statutory and GNWT bodies in communities, along with
320 special-purpose bodies in communities that have no tax
base. The latter alone, according to the report, were costing
over $66 million a year, money that it argued could be better
spent on health and education. A November 1991 report by
the government's financial management board, *Strength at Two
Levels*, agreed that "the GNWT has created too many non--
essential boards and agencies." It recommended that the territorial government increase its efficiency by transferring more
of its powers to the community level.

Some good things have resulted from the transfer of power
to the territorial government. Aboriginal culture and language
have become a part of northern government—although initially, Aboriginal people viewed the Yellowknife government
as opposed to their interests. In a move of symbolic importance
for Aboriginal residents, the GNWT obtained authority over
place names in the north, a power that the provinces have had
since the 1960s. This was important to many northern residents
because the place names they use are often at variance with
those used by federal authorities—in most cases to honour
European Arctic explorers and their patrons, or southern
political leaders. The first name change occurred in 1987 when
Frobisher Bay became Iqaluit, meaning "the place of fish" in
Inuktitut. Others continue to be made through public consultation.

In 1984, the Territorial Assembly adopted English and
French as the official languages and Inuktitut, Chipewyan,

Cree, Dogrib, Gwich'in, North Slavey and South Slavey as official Aboriginal languages. New language legislation adopted in the spring of 1990 made all Aboriginal languages official languages of the Territories, allowing them to be used in the legislature and the courts. The new legislation also allows people to deal with government in their Aboriginal language in areas where there is "significant demand." Government documents and notices may also be published in any of the official Aboriginal languages.

While there is official recognition for Aboriginal languages, many people are concerned that they have still not penetrated the bureaucracy. Former MLA Peter Ernerk, speaking in the Assembly, had this complaint:

> When a unilingual Inuit person from a community attempts to phone a government office, he or she is not always able to receive assistance in our language. Over the past four years I have phoned government offices on a number of occasions and attempted to speak Inuktitut. Many times I have received the answer, "I am sorry, I do not speak Inuktitut." ... Inuktitut is not being used whenever possible, even though it has been declared an official language of the NWT.

It is into these conditions that Nunavut will be born. Nunavut may have to deal with some very tough economic and social conditions not of its making. It will have to deal with them at a high administrative cost, and at the same time will have to cope with the pressures put on it by resource development. In spite of this, the Inuit remain convinced that Nunavut can make a difference to Inuit social conditions. Already plenty of work has been done to lay the groundwork for Nunavut.

4

Dividing the North

While Canadians have accepted the NWT as one of the political entities of the Canadian federation, it needs to be remembered that historically the NWT was simply territory kept in a holding pattern while the federal government decided what to do with it. There is no historical evidence to support the proposition that the Territories (either as they were in 1870 or as they are today) were intended to be a permanent political unit. In fact their history has been one of division for the purpose of creating new political units. Since the acquisition of the North West in 1870, the federal government has cut away at the territory to create new provinces (Alberta and Saskatchewan), expand other provinces (Manitoba, Ontario and Quebec) and create an additional territory (the Yukon).

The arguments advanced a hundred years ago, when Saskatchewan and Alberta were created, sound remarkably like those advanced today in the debate over division of the current NWT. "The desire for division was simply founded upon local ambitions for capital establishment," declared Sir Frederick Haultain, NWT premier in 1898. He characterized those who wanted to divide the Territories as "Little Westerners." The Territorial Assembly, by then based in Regina, was calling for autonomy, but there was sharp division as to how many provinces should be created out of the districts of Athabaska, Alberta, Saskatchewan and Assiniboia—four of the eight districts that composed the NWT (the northern districts were ignored in this debate). Proposals ranged from one province to three, and there were even those who wanted the west divided by a line running east-west just south of Saskatoon. Proponents of this division argued that the grain-growing flat and treeless southern prairies had a community of interests distinct from the north with its mixed farming and smaller holdings. At the same time, there were those who advocated that the District of Assiniboia (southern Saskatchewan) join Manitoba. The territorial government favoured one province, in the face of considerable opposition from Prince Albert, Edmonton and Calgary. In defending legislation to create the two provinces of Alberta and Saskatchewan from the NWT, Prime Minister Wilfrid Laurier stated that one province created from the whole territory would be too hard to govern. The Inuit take a similar position today.

Seven years after the creation of the two prairie provinces in 1912, further cuts were made from the Territories to extend the provinces of Manitoba, Ontario and Quebec to their current size. These extensions were conditional upon those provinces undertaking to settle outstanding Inuit and Indian claims in those districts. What was left of the Territories became the NWT as it now stands.

Shortly after World War II there was some discussion in academic circles of the future of the NWT. C. C. Lingard, in a 1946 article in the *Canadian Journal of Economics and Political Science*, proposed options that included extending the western provinces northward and creating a new province out of the Yukon and the Mackenzie District of the NWT.

Territorial Division in the Diefenbaker-Pearson Era

The question of division surfaced again in January 1962 when the NWT Council passed a resolution, spearheaded by Knut Lang, asking for the western territory to be separated from the eastern Arctic. The resolution stated:

> Whereas the ... increasing activity in the exploration for and development of mineral and petroleum resources in the Northwest Territories are bringing about rapid growth and change especially in the western portion ... And whereas the western region of the territories is a natural economic and social entity, which is now capable of more rapid development towards responsible government than the eastern and far northern regions ... Therefore, the Council ... resolves that the commissioner request the Minister of Northern Affairs and Natural Resources to recommend to the government of Canada that legislation be placed before the Parliament of Canada to

establish two new territories ... Mackenzie should com-
prise that part of the mainland of the present Northwest
Territories and associated islands lying west of the 105th
meridian of longitude, together with Banks and Victoria
islands ...

Mackenzie, then, would have comprised the western part of
the NWT. The resolution called for a nine-member council for
Mackenzie, of whom five would be elected, to govern from a
capital within the territory. For the other new territory, which
the resolution did not name, the council proposed that all
members of its council be appointed and that the seat of
government remain in Ottawa. Further, the resolution called
for a commissioner for the eastern Arctic who was to be an
officer of the Department of Northern Affairs. In short, the
resolution proposed self-government for the west and continued colonialism for the east. It also put most of the known
petroleum reserves in the west.

According to Bob Williamson, a University of Saskatchewan
anthropology professor who spent many years in the north
and who was living in Rankin Inlet as a freelance researcher
at the time, the council that passed the resolution was dominated by small businesspeople of the Mackenzie area. In their
minds, the backward east was hindering the economic
development of the west.

Meanwhile, the north had taken on a new importance in
Canadian thinking during the Diefenbaker years, as "the last
frontier." Diefenbaker's "road to resources" policy was a central campaign theme in the 1958 election:

What better preparation for the hundredth anniversary of
Confederation could there be than to spend the last decade of our first century as a nation in concentrating on
the development of that sparsely populated but tempting
four-fifths of our national territory that makes up the
Canadian North?

In view of Diefenbaker's interest in the north, it was not surprising that territorial division would receive support from his
government. So its September 1962 throne speech promised:

Measures will be placed before you to provide for the division of the Northwest Territories into two territories, and to provide more self-government for the residents of that area as a step toward the ultimate creation of new provinces in Canada's great north.

The fall of the Diefenbaker government did not change federal support for division. In 1963, after Diefenbaker's defeat, the Pearson government introduced legislation to create the Mackenzie Territory out of the west, and Nunassiaq—an Inuit word which means "the beautiful land"—out of the eastern Arctic. Bob Williamson recalls northerners receiving a letter asking them to select from a list of names the one they would like for their new territory. However, the final decision was made by officials in Ottawa, which, he says, infuriated many northerners. The failure to consult northerners as plans for Nunassiaq were developed would eventually kill the legislation.

Under Pearson's proposed legislation, the two territories were to be treated differently. Mackenzie was to have a council of nine members, five of whom were to be elected. Fort Smith (and not Yellowknife) was to be the capital. Nunassiaq was to have a council of seven, only two of them elected. Only one of the five appointees had to be a resident of the territory. The site of its capital was to be chosen by Ottawa. As in the Lang resolution of 1962, the NWT was to be divided along the 105th meridian from the middle of the Saskatchewan boundary to the Arctic Ocean, and Victoria and Banks islands were to be included in Mackenzie.

John Turner, the parliamentary secretary to the Minister of Northern Affairs, was given the job of shepherding the legislation through Parliament. But opposition to the proposal mounted for two reasons. First, there was the lack of consultation with the people of the eastern Arctic, and second, the fact that under the proposal the east would largely remain a powerless colony of Ottawa.

The Conservative MP for the north (at the time all of the NWT was represented by one MP), Gene Rheaume, broke ranks with his party to oppose the bill. He lobbied successfully for the committee considering the legislation to hear from northern witnesses, who included Williamson and Judge John

H.(Jack) Sissons, the first judge of the NWT Territorial Court. Also speaking out against the plan were the Chamber of Commerce of Frobisher Bay, the Cambridge Bay Municipal Council and the West Baffin Eskimo Co-operative. In the end, the committee heard strong arguments against division and the legislation never went back to the House.

The Carrothers Commission

The Territorial Council relented in its call for division and instead called for a commission to study the idea. So in June 1965 the Pearson government appointed a federal commission—the Advisory Commission on the Development of Government in the Northwest Territories—to study constitutional development in the north. Headed by Fred Carrothers, at the time dean of law at the University of Western Ontario, the commission also included Jean Beetz, who later became a Supreme Court of Canada judge, and John Parker, who later served for twelve years as deputy commissioner and ten years as commissioner of the NWT. This commission was the first federal body to travel through the north to hear from northerners.

The major recommendation of the commission, which reported in 1967, was that the responsibility for the administration of the NWT be gradually transferred to the Territorial Council and that Yellowknife, rather than Fort Smith, be established as the permanent seat of government. This would involve the establishment of a territorial civil service and the transfer of northern administrative headquarters from Ottawa to Yellowknife. The commission recommended, however, that Ottawa continue to hold responsibility for resource and economic development. A commissioner holding the rank of a federal deputy minister was to head the government, and a deputy commissioner was to be chosen from Council; these offices would evolve into positions equivalent to provincial lieutenant-governor and premier over a period of time. The commission further recommended that municipal-type government be implemented for communities in the NWT. Finally, the commission recommended against division of the Territories, but that the progress in developing home rule in the north be reviewed in ten years. These recommendations were accepted by Ottawa, and later that year some seventy-five government employees arrived by chartered DC-7 from Ottawa to run the territorial government.

But the idea of division did not die. In 1976 the Inuit Tapirisat of Canada put forward a proposal for settlement of their land claim along with the creation of Nunavut. The Inuit fleshed out their ideas for Nunavut in their sixty-page proposal entitled *Nunavut: A Proposal for the Settlement of Inuit Lands in the Northwest Territories,* which was presented to the federal government in February 1976. That proposal reiterated the Inuit position that land claims and political development are tied together and should be negotiated as one package. The Inuit, like other Aboriginal people, see land as part of the larger whole that is part of life itself. Land is part of the community. Therefore, to separate land rights from political rights was to them artificial. (The federal government position was based on historic notions of property law, under which property is something separate and apart from the community.) Nunavut was to be a trilingual government with almost the same powers as the NWT government. In addition, the Inuit claimed ownership of 650,000 square kilometres (in 1990 they accepted 350,000 square kilometres); a percentage of royalties from all resource development (not just developments on Inuit lands); and the exclusive right to hunt bear, marine mammals and musk-ox.

This proposal was eventually withdrawn because it had been drawn up without extensive community involvement and primarily by white consultants (mostly lawyers) working for the Inuit Tapirisat in Ottawa. But the Inuit quest for Nunavut continued unabated. The Prime Minister's office, however, was cool to the idea:

Legislative authority and governmental jurisdiction are not allocated in Canada on grounds that differentiate between the people on the basis of race.... Jurisdiction is placed in the hands of governments that are responsible directly or indirectly to the people—again without regard to race. These are the principles that the Government considers it essential to maintain for any political regime or governmental structure in the Northwest Territories.

The Drury Report

Prime Minister Pierre Trudeau did agree to a further study of constitutional development in the NWT and in August 1977 he appointed Bud Drury, a Liberal MP and former federal cabinet minister and territorial councillor, as his special representative to

> conduct a systematic consultation with recognized leaders of the Territorial Government ... and native groups about specific measures for modifying and improving existing structures, institutions and systems of government ... with a view to extending representative, responsive and effective government to all parts of the Territories and at the same time accommodating the legitimate interests of all groups in northern society, beginning with those of the Indian, Inuit and Métis.

His terms of reference asked him to consult with and seek a consensus among northern people on, among other issues, "possible division of the Northwest Territories ... and transfer and delegation of Federal responsibilities and programs to the Territorial Governments."

In his December 1979 report, Drury concluded:

> The longer-term external consequences of division have not yet been adequately examined. The proponents of division have not examined as thoroughly the constraints on autonomy in the realpolitik of federal-provincial relations as they have the weaknesses of current government in the NWT.... The conclusions that follow in this report will support a united NWT.

Drury, however, did not reject division outright. He suggested that it needed further study and recommended that a separate forum—a constitutional convention or constituent assembly— be elected to advise the Territorial Council on the issue. Included in Drury's recommendations was a process to educate people on issues surrounding division and the holding of a referendum on any recommendations of the forum. Native aspirations, he concluded, could be met by settling land claims and setting aside land for Native peoples.

The Inuit Tapirisat of Canada quickly challenged Drury's conclusions. In a letter sent to Prime Minister Trudeau early in 1980, ITC president Michael Amarook wrote: "We reject Mr. Drury's view that the concerns of the Inuit of Nunavut can be adequately protected through ownership of small pockets of reserved land." The letter went on to criticize the Drury report's recommendation of further transfer of power to the territorial government before the question of a new territory had been dealt with. The Inuit also objected to the process, which separated constitutional development from the settlement of land claims.

Some members of Parliament were also unhappy with Drury's report. In early May 1980 both Warren Allmand and Peter Ittinuar, the first Inuk elected to Parliament and the first MP from the newly created eastern Arctic seat of Nunatsiaq, introduced private members' bills to divide the Territories. Like most private members' bills, these never got past the first reading stage.

A New Inuit Proposal and a Territory-Wide Initiative

Three years after submitting its first proposals for Nunavut to the Trudeau government, the ITC adopted the position paper *Political Development in Nunavut* at its 1979 annual meeting in Igloolik. This document proposed a fifteen-year period in which the eastern Arctic would proceed to eventual provincehood. In a three-stage plan for development the Inuit proposed, first, the recognition of Nunavut; second, the transfer of territorial powers to the new territory; and finally, the conversion of Nunavut into a province. The paper also rejected the option of a regional government for the eastern Arctic within the GNWT as being too cumbersome, in that it would have imposed four layers of government on a sparse population, whereas people in southern Canada only contend with three (municipal, provincial and federal). The concept of some sort of home rule option was also rejected as being outside the current federal arrangement.

At the same time the Legislative Assembly (the new name that the Territorial Assembly had adopted) published a position paper in which it called for the devolution of power to the existing NWT government, with the eventual acquisition of provincial status. The question of division was to be left for later, with possible resolution through a referendum.

The territorial elections in 1979 brought about a major change in the Assembly. Aboriginal groups, who until then had boycotted the territorial electoral process because it was in their view an institution unsympathetic to their views, decided to participate actively in those elections. The result was a majority of MLAs of Aboriginal ancestry. Aboriginal issues assumed a new importance in the Assembly. It appointed a committee on unity in November 1979. A year later the committee reported, finding no support for the status quo, and recommended division and called for a vote on the issue. The Assembly then voted unanimously to hold a territorial plebiscite (as opposed to a binding referendum).

A lobby group formed to promote the idea of division, along with a new constitutional framework for the north originating in the north. Composed of members of the Legislative Assembly and representatives of each of the major Aboriginal constituencies in the NWT (the Métis, Dene, Inuit and Inuvialuit), in 1982 the lobby group took the name Constitutional Alliance of the Northwest Territories. The group pledged itself to support division and to work for a Yes vote in the upcoming plebiscite.

That plebiscite was held on April 14, 1982. Voters were asked: "Do you think that the Northwest Territories should be divided?" Of the 18,962 eligible voters, 9,891 voted; 5,560 (56 percent) supported division. An analysis of the vote tells of the extent to which Nunavut was supported by residents of the eastern Arctic. The turnout in the east was 75 percent as compared to 45 percent in the west. Eighty-two percent of the voters in the east supported division; in the western Arctic (the Mackenzie Delta area) the figure was 44 percent in favour, and in western Aboriginal communities it was 60 percent. In western non-Aboriginal communities, 25 percent supported division. After the results were in, the Assembly voted 19 to 0 in favour of division and called on the federal government to appoint a boundaries commission to recommend the new boundaries after consultation with the people of the NWT.

At a July 1982 meeting of the Constitutional Alliance, it was agreed that two additional forums be set up: one for the east, to be called the Nunavut Constitutional Forum (NCF) and one for the west to be called the Western Constitutional Forum (WCF). These new forums were to carry out tasks that included developing a clear position on the new boundary, developing proposals and new constitutions for the new governments, ensuring public participation in the development of the new constitutions and negotiating the final proposals with Ottawa. Each of the new forums was to have at least one non-Aboriginal MLA to represent the non-Aboriginal population. The Alliance also agreed that the Inuvialuit of the Mackenzie Delta could participate in either forum. The Constitutional Alliance was to continue its work as a mediator between the two forums and also as a vehicle for public education on constitutional development.

The Western Constitutional Forum held its first meeting in September 1982. The Nunavut Constitutional Forum held its first meeting shortly thereafter. The NCF included eastern Arctic MLAs along with representatives of various Inuit groups, and was chaired by Dennis Patterson. It produced a number of position papers after extensive consultation with eastern Arctic communities through meetings and discussions published in newspapers and broadcast on radio and television. The most extensive position papers were the 1983 working document, *Building Nunavut*, which was taken into every community by the NCF that fall for consultation and refinement, and the revised version of 1985, *Building Nunavut: Today and Tomorrow*. In the 1987 Iqaluit Agreement signed by the NCF and WCF some of its principles were expanded upon. The heart of that agreement was the drawing of a tentative boundary line between Nunavut and the rest of the NWT. But the agreement also set out the principles on which Nunavut and Denendeh (the name suggested by some commentators for the western half of the NWT) would operate.

While the NCF was drafting proposals for the government of Nunavut, the WCF was doing the same for the western part of the territory. The status of the Aboriginal community in the western Territories differs substantially from that in the east. The Inuit, who are a majority in the east, are a relatively homogeneous population and have no large cities. In the west,

Aboriginal people are a significant portion of the population, but do not form the majority. Much of the western population is in Yellowknife, a non-Aboriginal community. So too, the Aboriginal community is divided between the Métis and the Dene, and within the Dene community there are several linguistic and cultural groups. The WCF proposals ranged from exclusive Aboriginal governments within the territory, to a central government with exclusive Aboriginal municipalities, to a public government with guaranteed Aboriginal influence but not control.

Under one proposal developed by the WCF, Denendeh—"the land of the people" in the Dene language—would have become a province or a territory similar to a province. However, unlike other provinces, it would have guarantees to ensure the survival of the Dene nation. Thus the Dene argued that Denendeh should have power over fisheries and navigable waters (areas of federal jurisdiction) to "ensure protection of the aquatic environment of Denendeh which is basic to our traditional Dene way of life" and also control over employment and labour in order to "preserve and develop historical Dene work styles and employment relations." Decisions in Denendeh would have resulted from consensuses reached in community meetings and referendums held to ensure that decisions were widely based. The Charter of Founding Principles for Denendeh would have included entrenchment of Aboriginal languages as official languages. No matter what the Dene population was they would be guaranteed a minimum of 30 percent of the seats on community councils and in the legislative assembly. There would be a Dene Senate, composed entirely of Dene, which would have the power to veto any legislation that adversely affected Aboriginal rights.

The work of the WCF was gradually supplanted by the Dene/Métis land claims negotiations. Under the Dene/Métis Comprehensive Land Claim Agreement in Principle, which never became finalized—because some communities disagreed with a clause requiring the surrender of Aboriginal rights—the Dene and Métis would have been given an opportunity to participate in various resource management boards.

Once again, the federal government came to accept the idea of division. In November 1982, Indian Affairs Minister John

Munro announced that the federal cabinet had approved the idea, on the condition that outstanding land claims be settled, there be continued support for division by the residents of the NWT, the parties agree on a dividing line and there be an agreement on the division of powers between local, regional and territorial governments.

The Federal and Territorial Governments Prepare for Division

Both the federal and territorial governments commissioned consultants' studies on the possibility of division. The Legislative Assembly commissioned its first study in 1981. A more comprehensive study followed in 1983, prepared by M. Whittington and Sheila MacPherson for the Assembly's Sub-Committee on Division. It detailed the kinds of administrative questions that would have to be dealt with if division occurred. For example, it concluded that staffing requirements for Nunavut would exceed staffing required by the NWT government to service Nunavut; therefore, it would be necessary to train the local Inuit to fill positions in the bureaucracy. The consultants concluded that few NWT civil servants would transfer to the Nunavut government.

Although the report conceded that the location of the capital was a political question, it listed several non-political factors which should be considered. Those included the presence of the best existing infrastructure so as to reduce start-up costs, a central location to make it accessible to all settlements and the best flying weather (the fewest snow storms and fog).

At the same time the federal government commissioned a study on the cost of transition. It concluded that the direct cost would be $66.8 million in 1984 dollars and that at most 10 to 20 percent of GNWT employees would transfer to the government of Nunavut. Of the three models of transition considered, a long-term controlled transition over a period of thirteen to twenty years would ensure that the maximum number of government jobs would go to qualified Inuit. In short, time would give Inuit people the opportunity to develop the skills needed to run a modern government.

John Munro's support for division became entrenched as government policy. In his opening remarks to the 1984 Constitutional Conference on Aboriginal Rights, Pierre Trudeau declared:

> The great majority of the Inuit, … who live in the eastern Arctic, are also engaged in the land claims settlement process. In the matter of self-government their aspirations, however, are very different. They look to division of the Northwest Territories setting up in the eastern part they call Nunavut a public or non-ethnic government on the model of a territorial government. The government of Canada has agreed in principle to the division of the Northwest Territories and is ready to give favourable consideration to those Inuit proposals.

A year later an optimistic Minister of Indian Affairs, David Crombie, representing the newly elected Conservative government, told the NWT Legislative Assembly: "I believe it to be the common resolve of all of us, that the Parliament of Canada transform the Northwest Territories into two new territories by … 1987." Crombie even dropped the earlier federal condition that land claims be settled before division.

Division didn't occur in 1987. But that year the Western Constitutional Forum and the NCF reached an agreement—the Iqaluit Agreement—on the boundary (which later was rejected by many western communities) and which confirmed the "establishment of two distinct political jurisdictions; an eastern region to be called Nunavut and a western region which is as yet unnamed." The Assembly accepted the agreement and called for a territory-wide plebiscite for May 20, 1987, had the agreement been ratified by the constituent communities.

In the fall of 1989 Peter Ernerk brought the subject of division to the Legislative Assembly floor again, noting that the 11th Legislative Assembly had not yet spoken on the question of Nunavut. His motion called for the Assembly to "affirm its support for the creation of a Nunavut Territory." The resolution was approved by a vote of 20 to 0, with one abstention.

In his delivery of the equivalent of a throne speech, Territorial Commissioner Dan Norris told the opening of the Assembly in early 1991 that the government remained committed to the creation of Nunavut and "as a result, division of the territories is once again on the top of the agenda with land claims, devolution and other issues." The territorial executive council—which functions as a cabinet—agreed. Two weeks later it tabled a position paper on political and constitutional development that called the creation of Nunavut a major priority.

A further study on division was released in late 1991. Commissioned by the government of the Northwest Territories, the Coopers & Lybrand study looked at the financial impact of division. The report concluded that additional annual operating costs of two territories (instead of one) would be $86,869,000 or 9.6 percent over and above the current costs of government in the NWT. There would be transitional costs (dealing with relocation and severance of personnel, legal issues surrounding conversion of laws and regulations, transferring management and dividing inventory) and infrastructure costs (developing a new capital in the east). Considering these factors the report concluded that the net annual cost would range from $161,303,000 to $184,506,000. In estimating annual costs, the cost of building a new capital— $520 to $587 million, depending on the site—were spread out over a twenty-year period. Iqaluit was deemed the least expensive, followed by Rankin Inlet, and then by Cambridge Bay.

The report also considered the effect division would have on government jobs. It estimated that there would be a need for 250 fewer government positions in Yellowknife and nearly 1,200 new jobs in Nunavut. As a result, the centre chosen as capital could expect to face a population increase of between 4,000 and 4,500.

In reaching its conclusions Coopers & Lybrand did not consider additional costs which would result from responsibilities arising out of future land claims settlements or arising from the further devolution of federal powers to the territorial governments. The report also did not consider additional costs which might arise if the Nunavut government operated in a highly decentralized fashion.

At the time of writing the federal government had also commissioned a major study to look at the cost implications of division.

Both in anticipation of the land claims agreement becoming final and as a result of the 1990 agreement-in-principle a great many government bodies have been set up. In June of 1989 Indian Affairs Minister Pierre Cadieux and NWT Renewable Resources Minister Titus Allooloo appointed the Nunavut Planning Commission to undertake responsibility for land use planning in the Nunavut area. The commission was given the responsibility for monitoring the implementation of the Lancaster Sound Land Use Plan.

In mid-1990, the newly formed Nunavut Wildlife Advisory Board began its work by rejecting a Department of Fisheries recommendation of a ten-year moratorium on hunting beluga whales. Instead it recommended that the quota be reduced from ninety whales per year to fifteen. Local hunters, supported by Dennis Patterson, government leader and MLA for Iqaluit, questioned the validity of the new recommendation, made without consulting them. Patterson addressed a public letter to the federal Fisheries Minister, Bernard Valcourt. He suggested that the board was influenced too much by the strong advice of departmental officials and didn't consider local interests.

Tungavik Federation of Nunavut president Paul Quassa, in a letter to the *Nunatsiaq News*, went to great lengths to distance the existing Wildlife Advisory Board from the Nunavut Wildlife Management Board (NWMB) required to be appointed once a final agreement is ratified between the government and the Inuit.

> The Nunavut Wildlife Management Advisory Board is not TFN's Board.... It is an interim ... Board.... It was established because both Inuit and government needed a temporary vehicle for talking to each other about wildlife ... The NWMB will not be like the existing advisory board.... It will have its own support staff and researchers ... to make informed decisions acceptable to communities.... Inuit hunters will be relied upon and encouraged to participate fully.

But, as Quassa conceded, the new board to be appointed under the lands claims agreement will make mistakes, too. Self-government does not mean perfect community harmony. It does mean the right to make your own mistakes.

The Nunavut Trust, the body that is to receive the cash compensation under the agreement and the Inuit share of resource revenue, has also been set up.

In December 1991 the TFN and the federal government announced that they had finalized the Nunavut land claims agreement, subject to ratification by the Inuit beneficiaries. It was as part of that package that the federal government announced that it would introduce legislation in the fall of 1992 to divide the Territories and to put in place the government of Nunavut several years later.

Paul Quassa contends that once the final agreement is in place there won't be much of a role for the GNWT in the Nunavut region. "The bodies created by the agreement override the territorial jurisdiction; therefore, what is there for the territorial government to do?" he asks. "With all the management boards [to be put in place under the agreement] we *de facto* have Nunavut."

5

Obstacles to Nunavut

Questions and Objections

While the concept of Nunavut has received strong support in the eastern Arctic, other voices have been more guarded. Even many Aboriginal voices have questioned division.

"The Inuvialuit remain fundamentally opposed to the issue of division at this particular time," Roger Gruben, director of the Inuvialuit Regional Council, told the NWT Legislative Assembly on October 31, 1989. He expressed concern that division would jeopardize plans by Shell, Gulf and Esso to ship natural gas along the proposed Mackenzie Valley pipeline. It is a position that Gruben has often repeated. "Division is not the right thing at this time," he told the author in a 1990 interview. On the eve of the plebiscite, however, he softened his stand.

"It's an issue which is lying low right now ... we voted for it last fall, they can't say we denied their aspirations ... but the same time we're not pushing it," was how Yellowknife MLA Tony Whitford, himself a Métis, summed up the situation in mid-1990.

The Dene and Métis people of the western NWT have often expressed concerns about Nunavut. They see Nunavut as intruding on some of their traditional territory. There is also speculation that the Dene fear that with division Aboriginal people will no longer form the majority in the western territory and hence Aboriginal issues will not be at the top of the political agenda.

Even the Inuit of the Kitikmeot region (in the central Arctic) are not as certain about Nunavut as are their eastern kin. "I've never heard people talk about it here or at meeting," an official of the Kitikmeot Inuit Association said. TFN leaders and eastern MLAs agree that they need to do more to reach out to the residents of Kitikmeot and make them feel comfortable with the idea of Nunavut.

"Nunavut is an outdated idea, one of the last applications of the postwar ideal of national self-determination," University of Alberta political scientist Gurston Dacks wrote in a 1986 *Canadian Public Policy* article, "The Case Against Dividing the Northwest Territories." Dacks raised a number of fundamental questions that will have to be answered by both northerners and Canadians as a whole. He argued that division of the Territories would weaken the territorial voice in national affairs, divide the Aboriginal voice in the north and harm the fiscal position of the NWT. He further suggested that Nunavut would end up with a weakened civil service or one dominated by whites. Finally, Dacks argued that Nunavut could not truly speak for the Inuit. It would be a public government and would have to speak for all Nunavut residents, not only the 80 percent of its population who would be Inuit.

The arguments advanced by Dacks still have to be dealt with. Other major problems as well have plagued the quest for Nunavut. The boundary issue—where to draw the line between east and west—has been a part of the northern political scene since division was first proposed and has consumed considerable time, energy and resources. It may yet scuttle Nunavut. A related question has been whether the Mackenzie Delta area should be a part of Nunavut, though the current consensus is that the western Arctic would remain a part of the new western territory. The effect of devolution of power to the GNWT must also be considered. Would a territorial government strengthened by a further devolution of powers be willing to give up control over land, resources and some of its budget? Difficult constitutional questions arise, too. No longer can Ottawa create new provinces unilaterally, as a result of the 1982 constitution. But can Ottawa create a new territory without the approval of the provinces? Finally, there are economic questions to be answered. Critics argue that with its high birth rate and unemployment rate, and with little immediate prospect for economic development, the eastern Arctic simply isn't a viable territory. And at this time of economic restraint, can Canada afford two territories—at an additional annual cost of nearly $200 million—both dependent on the national treasury?

Aboriginal Voice and Representation

One argument against division can be dealt with fairly quickly. It is true that division would weaken the territorial voice in national affairs. However, at the same time it has to be recognized that that territorial voice has never been very strong: the NWT has had observer status, if that, at federal-provincial conferences.

It is not true that dividing the territory would weaken the unity of northern Aboriginal people. That argument is based on the assumption that there is one Aboriginal voice in the north. There isn't. The Inuit have disagreed with the Inuvialuit over the creation of Nunavut. The Inuvialuit, who once advanced their land claim with the Inuit of the eastern Arctic, broke away in 1977 and signed their own agreement in 1984. The Dene and Métis have debated the Inuit for years over the location of the boundary between east and west. Within the Dene and Métis camp itself there have been sharp disputes over the final agreement on their land claim, resulting in the eventual rejection of the agreement. Some communities within the Dene camp have now signed their own land claims agreements.

The fact that northern Aboriginal groups do not speak with one voice is not surprising. In the south, the Manitoba Métis disagreed with other Aboriginal groups over the Meech Lake Accord. The leadership of the Saskatchewan Federation of Indian Nations publicly disagreed with the tactics employed at Oka, Quebec, by the Mohawk Indians. Nor does one see such unity in the non-Aboriginal community. The people of Saskatchewan do not speak with one voice. To suggest that division will destroy the northern Aboriginal voice is to base one's argument on a myth. There is no single northern Aboriginal voice, nor is it realistic to expect people with different cultures, languages and history living in very different parts of the country to speak with one voice.

In light of this, we should ask what political arrangement would most effectively represent these diverse voices. Right now, only a third of the NWT population are Inuit. However, the majority population of Nunavut would be Inuit; therefore, that government would be in a much better position to bring Inuit issues to national attention. It is true that a Nunavut government would speak for all its residents, but it would have a special responsibility—much like Quebec's special responsibility—to defend and protect the interests of its majority constituency, the Inuit.

The Boundary Question

"I see this boundary dispute as quite pivotal ... in allowing us to get on with the work of constitutional development in the Territories ... that process stops and is dead when the boundary agreement hasn't been reached," NWT government leader Dennis Patterson said in a July 1990 address to the NWT Métis Association.

Determining the location of the boundary between Nunavut and the rest of the territory has been a stumbling block on the road to division. In view of the time and energy that has gone into the issue one can almost speculate that the issue has been used by opponents of division to delay or derail the move to division. However, in fairness, the boundary issue involves a great many complex questions. Should the treeline (a diagonal line running across the territory) form the boundary or should there be a north-south line running north from the Manitoba-Saskatchewan border, in a manner similar to that proposed by the Pearson government? Into which territory should the Mackenzie Delta-Beaufort Sea area, the western Kitikmeot communities (Coppermine, Cambridge Bay, Bay Chimo and Bathurst Inlet) fall? How should the oil and gas resources of the western Arctic be divided? Which Aboriginal community should have the benefit of the game resources of the Contwoyto Lake area and the Thelon Game Sanctuary?

The Dene/Métis and the Inuit began negotiations in the early 1980s. From 1982 to 1987 much of the boundary work was carried out by the Western Constitutional Forum, the Nunavut Constitutional Forum and the Constitutional Alliance. Later, the boundary issue was taken over by the TFN and the Dene/Métis Joint Negotiating Secretariat. In their first proposals, the Inuit argued that the treeline should form the border.

This border poses a number of problems. First, the treeline is not a constant line, but one that moves with climatic changes. More important, there are Dene communities near the line who use the land north of the line as their hunting grounds. Both the long-disputed Contwoyto Lake area—claimed by the Dogrib and Sahtu Indians as well as by the Kitikmeot Inuit—and the Thelon Game Sanctuary are north of the treeline.

In a 1979 decision relating to Keewatin Inuit claims to the Baker Lake area, Judge Mahoney of the Federal Court Trial Division relied heavily on the evidence of two archaeologists, Dr. Elmer Harp of Dartmouth College in New Hampshire, and Dr. J. V. Wright of the National Museum of Man. In the summer of 1958 Harp had examined forty-two sites in the Thelon River country west of Baker Lake. Of the sites he was able to classify, he concluded that six were prehistoric Inuit and eighteen were Indian sites. Mahoney ruled that some of the area southwest of Baker Lake area had been used by the Dene people and was not exclusive Inuit territory:

> During the prehistoric period Indians occupied the Dubaunt Valley and both Indians and Inuit occupied portions of the Thelon Valley.... The evidence suggests that, in prehistoric times, the southwest portion of the Area was a transitional zone with primarily Indian occupation toward the boreal forest and primarily Inuit occupation toward Baker Lake.

Mahoney's judgment adds strength to the Dene claim (which the Dogrib and Sahtu Indians are part of) that some of the area north of the treeline was their traditional territory.

The treeline as a border would also place the Mackenzie Delta–Beaufort Sea area (including Aklavik, Inuvik and Tuktoyaktuk) in Nunavut. The 2,500 Inuvialuit of this area share language and culture with the eastern Inuit (though they are believed to have arrived in Canada much more recently then their eastern counterparts), but their economic and transportation systems are tied to the western NWT. Most western residents of the NWT want this area in their jurisdiction, because the Mackenzie River was part of their traditional transportation system and because of the oil in the area.

According to a 1984 study, over 90 percent of the known oil and gas reserves of the NWT would fall within Nunavut if the Mackenzie Delta–Beaufort Sea area were included in Nunavut.

If the Beaufort were included in the west, the known oil and gas potential would be split between the two territories.

Initially, COPE (the organization representing the Inuvialuit) decided to join the NCF, provided it was guaranteed a regional government. But as representatives from both the NCF and the WCF toured the western Arctic communities, it was clear that loyalties in the area were divided. At length, at a January 1985 meeting, agreement was reached within the Constitutional Alliance that the Inuvialuit should be in the western territory. A semi-autonomous regional municipality was proposed by the WCF as a means of ensuring that the Inuvialuit could preserve their language and culture.

The agreement also left it open to communities in the western Kitikmeot (Coppermine, Cambridge Bay, Bay Chimo and Bathurst Inlet) to choose which territory they wanted to be in. According to Dan O'Neill, GNWT Assistant Regional Director of the area, western Kitikmeot has many ties to the Inuvik area. Many of the Inuit in Coppermine and Holman were initially reindeer herders in the Inuvik area. Today they use the medical facilities and schools in Inuvik. Their language is written in the Latin alphabet, as are the languages of the Mackenzie Delta area. Syllabics are used in the eastern Arctic.

The 1985 agreement was short lived. The Inuvialuit rejected the WCF proposal, and Legislative Assembly members from the east would not agree to truncate the original Nunavut and leave the Inuit under two separate jurisdictions.

A year later, in early May, negotiators from the Dene/Métis secretariat and the TFN reached a tentative deal on the boundary, which included an overlap area to be managed jointly by both jurisdictions. A more formal agreement on the boundary, the Iqaluit Agreement, was reached by Inuit and Dene/Métis negotiators in January 1987. The boundary line was to start at 103 degrees 10 minutes west on the Saskatchewan border, run due north for approximately 400 kilometres, then turn northwest and run to the eastern boundary of the Inuvialuit settlement area. The agreement put the Mackenzie Delta–Beaufort Sea area in the western territory. The western Kitikmeot communities fell within Nunavut. It also put much of the Thelon Game Sanctuary and Contwoyto Lake in Nunavut. Division was set for October 1, 1991.

The agreement was subject to ratification by the two claimant groups, by the Territorial Assembly and by a public plebiscite. Four Assembly members from the eastern Arctic continued to argue for the treeline as a boundary. In a 17 to 3 vote, with 3 abstentions, the Assembly approved the boundary and selected May 20, 1987, as the date for the plebiscite. April 1 was set as the date for the two constituencies (the members of the WCF and NCF) to approve the new boundary. The Inuit met that goal, but the WCF was not able to get approval from all its member communities on the boundary.

By 1990 the dispute had been narrowed to the Contwoyto Lake area, but still the parties could reach no final agreement. Nor could they agree on a framework for further discussions. According to Paul Quassa, with the failure of the Dene/Métis land claims agreement in early 1990 they had little incentive or interest to think about creating a Dene and Métis territory.

Eventually, federal Indian Affairs Minister Tom Siddon appointed former NWT Commissioner John Parker to come up with a single boundary line. Parker, who was accepted as arbitrator by both sides, suggested a line slightly further to the east than past proposals. His proposed line went well into the Thelon Game Sanctuary and gave the southern part of Contwoyto Lake to the western territory. While this boundary received Ottawa's approval, it was almost immediately rejected by the Dene/Métis.

The Inuit accepted Parker's proposal, however. It forms the basis of the boundary for the Nunavut land claims settlement area. It is this boundary that was proposed for a territorial vote of all residents on May 4, 1992.

In that vote, nearly 55 percent of the more than 15,000 people who voted supported the proposed boundary. Support for the boundary was particularly strong in the eastern Arctic, where over 91 percent of the voters agreed with the boundary. In the west, many voters abstained.

To complicate matters, the Chipewyan (Dene) from northern Manitoba and Saskatchewan have advanced a claim to some 24,000 square kilometres around Ennadai Lake, 75 kilometres north of the Saskatchewan/Manitoba boundary, territory that is also claimed by the Inuit. In December 1991 the Dene commenced a court action for a declaration that those lands were part of their treaty lands and also part of their traditional Aboriginal lands. Dene opponents in the NWT have also threatened action to block the proposed boundary. This opposition may yet derail the boundary; coupled with the close vote, it could always force the federal government to rethink its position. This might particularly be a risk if there is a change in the government.

Closely connected to the boundary issue is the question of what happens to the western half of the NWT. With the collapse of the Dene/Métis land talks there has been little incentive to work towards the creation of Denendeh. Several groups that made up the Dene/Métis coalition, such as the Gwich'in of the Mackenzie Delta, have pursued and signed their own land claims agreements. In its 1991 position paper on political and constitutional development the government announced a plan to develop a constitutional model for a new territory in the western NWT. A territorial commission was appointed to work on the model. These developments led to accusations from some Dene spokespersons that the government was turning its back on the idea of Denendeh and the work that had been done towards its creation. The government response was that the new western territory would include more than Dene and Métis people, it would include the Inuvialuit as well, and that the name "Denendeh" might not be appropriate. This uncertainty has meant that there is little pressure from the Dene community to resolve constitutional questions in the NWT with which the boundary question is intricately tied.

Devolution of Power to the GNWT

While the debate over where to put the boundary line continues, Ottawa has continued to transfer more powers to the territorial government. The Inuit have argued that devolution of powers to the GNWT will make it significantly more difficult to divide the Territories. Their position is that once powers are given to one government and structures put in place to exercise those powers, it becomes much more difficult to dismantle them. Once the GNWT has obtained powers approaching those of a province, will it want to give up some of those powers along with a substantial portion of its budget in order that Nunavut can be given life?

In the spring of 1990, the NWT government asked for Ottawa's co-operation in developing a framework to cover further devolution of powers and to ensure that any new Aboriginal institutions be developed in conformity to NWT legislation. It also asked for a transfer of land and water to the NWT by federal order-in-council.

Paul Quassa, TFN president, objected:

> It would be to the obvious risk of TFN and, given the history of unfulfilled treaty and other constitutional obligations in southern Canada, to the government of Canada, to conceive of a major transfer of beneficial control over resources to the Legislative Assembly prior to the resolution of the outstanding issue of Aboriginal land title.... Division still seems to be treated as some kind of add-on [to the process of devolution]. It is not appropriate to discuss "a" constitution, when the creation of Nunavut necessarily implies two constitutions.... TFN cannot support any amendments to the NWT Act that do not coincide with these two events.

His message is one that the Inuit have argued for several years. In her 1985–86 annual report, then ITC president Rhoda Innuksuk said:

> By giving increased responsibilities to Yellowknife, it is easier for the federal government to argue that Inuit needs are being addressed and that as such the Government of the Northwest Territories is the legitimate representative of the Inuit, thereby eliminating the need for Nunavut.

Her point is one that has been supported by other proponents of Nunavut and by political scientists. As the territorial government is given more powers it is in a better position to provide benefits and contracts to residents. As territorial residents gain more benefits they may be less inclined to support a new territorial government and more inclined to support the status quo. Given the fact that government is the biggest employer and biggest source of contracts in the north, its financial clout is very real.

The Inuit also argue that historical precedent supports their position. They point out that when the Prairie provinces were created their geographic limits were established before full provincial powers were devolved to them. In the NWT, however, many provincial-type powers are being acquired before the questions are settled of how many jurisdictions there will be and where their boundaries will be drawn.

Economic and Social Obstacles

The socio-economic situation in the eastern Arctic gives rise to two problems which will have to be dealt with if Nunavut is to become reality. First, how soon can the eastern Arctic produce a trained cadre of administrators to run the government? Second, with the many problems people there face, how will Nunavut pay the high cost of social services? Given current federal fiscal realities, a serious question arises as to whether Ottawa would be prepared to increase its northern support so that Nunavut could deal with its problems.

If Nunavut is to be truly representative of its people then it is important that it function in the Inuktitut language and have a significant proportion of Inuit in senior positions. At least two scholars have suggested that finding such people may be a problem in the foreseeable future. According to Gurston Dacks,

> within a very short period of time, a relatively large number of policy positions will have to be filled. However, Inuit candidates for these jobs will be hard to find. The overall pool of such people is small and not expanding substantially.

This was supported by Colin Irwin's 1988 study. He concluded:

> As long as current trends persist, most of the people living in the Arctic with professional and university qualifications will be white, and they will continue to dominate the higher levels of management in both the private and public sectors.

Irwin went on to examine whether there was a new generation of Inuit leadership developing.

The fear was also expressed to me, by some white staff
members of the Government of the Northwest Territories,
that the current Inuit leadership, now in their late 30's and
early 40's, does not appear to be in the process of being
strengthened by a new generation of younger leadership.
They felt the possible failure to create a new generation
of leadership had serious implications for the future
development of Inuit society.

Can one truly build a new government with a population
base that suffers a serious educational deficiency and numerous social problems? The TFN's answer is yes. They believe
that Nunavut can be the answer to the eastern Arctic's social
problems. They argue that management skills required to run
Nunavut will be developed as the land claims agreement is
implemented and the boards and commissions needed under
that agreement are developed.

"The experience of running post-settlement Inuit organizations would serve to create a large pool of Inuit leadership,
both to spearhead the campaign for Nunavut and to run it
once created," is the view expressed in *Nunavut: Political
Choices and Manifest Destiny*, commissioned by the TFN. The
TFN has already instituted a one-year training program, based
in Ottawa, to acquaint Inuit participants with land claims and
other issues, and with the workings of Inuit organizations and
government. Paul Quassa explained that the program was an
attempt to have more people ready to deal with the implementation of the agreement. "Once signed, we'll need all kinds of
people who know the agreement," he said.

In short, the Inuit believe that as more institutions result
from the land claims settlement there will be more jobs in the
eastern Arctic for Inuit, jobs now filled by people in Yellowknife and Ottawa, and by non-Inuit civil servants who have
been sent to the eastern Arctic. The creation of jobs will in turn
lead to the solution of other social problems, and, notably,
there will be more incentive for people to remain in school.

The proposed land claims settlement gives a clear advantage to the Inuit in seeking positions in government and on

boards set up under the agreement. Government departments are to have proportionate representation of Inuit on their staff and job qualifications are to include knowledge of Inuit language and culture. Boards set up under the agreement will be able to hear and accept submissions in Inuktitut, along with Canada's official languages. The latter requirement alone will provide significant work for translators.

Even without the land claims agreement, the territorial government has made significant efforts to bring Inuit into the public service. Forty-five percent of territorial employees in the Kitikmeot area and 66 percent in the Keewatin area are Inuit. Obviously, these are employees the Nunavut government could call upon to staff its service.

However, this dependence on public sector jobs raises the difficult question of how that public sector will be paid for. Is the federal government likely to pick up the tab? Of course, the federal government might well agree to division but simply divide the money allocated to the NWT into two packages. It should also be borne in mind that the federal government has already introduced a new funding formula which will have the effect of reducing payments to the NWT by some $100 million over five years (approximately 13 percent of the territorial budget). With the federal treasury running a huge annual deficit, the prospect of increasing federal expenditures in the north might not be realistic.

The issue of financing for Nunavut remains one of the major hurdles that has to be overcome. Reassuringly, on the eve of the boundary plebescite of May 4, 1992, the federal and territorial governments along with the TFN initialled a political accord, wherein Ottawa agreed to pick up the additional costs of the new government. At the same time, the federal minister in charge of Northern Affairs, Tom Siddon, stated he did not believe the costs would be as high as initially anticipated.

Obstacles to the Creation of a New Province

For some Inuit, provincehood is not the main question. Their goal is an Inuit homeland. Thomas Suluk, at the time an MP for the eastern Arctic, made the point in a 1987 debate on the Meech Lake Accord in the House of Commons:

If I have a criticism of the Special Joint Committee Report it is that the Northern Chapter thinks strictly in terms of provincial status.... [We want] arrangements which do not force Inuit into a southern mould. Nunavut is our answer. If the two Territories are so concerned about the issue of provincehood, there is a practical way to resolve it ... why not merge the Territory of the Yukon and the western part of the NWT to make one Territory and, consequently, an eleventh province? We could then have only one Territory left in the Canadian Confederation, a native territory [Nunavut] which could then become Canada's showcase to the world.

Others do not share Suluk's viewpoint. In its 1991 position paper on political and constitutional development, the executive of the NWT government stated that one of the main elements in its plan was "to ensure that both Nunavut and the new western Territory can seek and be granted provincial status."

"I see Nunavut as a province-in-waiting," then government leader Dennis Patterson said in the Assembly early in 1991. Addressing a 1990 workshop sponsored by TFN and the Canadian Arctic Resources Committee, Assistant Deputy Minister of Indian and Northern Affairs Richard Van Loon spoke for the federal government: "What we are doing in the north is creating provinces."

Until 1982, Ottawa could and did create new provinces. The federal government unilaterally created Manitoba in 1870, and Saskatchewan and Alberta in 1905. Prince Edward Island, British Columbia and Newfoundland were admitted by agreement between Ottawa and the appropriate colonial government. In 1898 the federal government unilaterally created the territory of Yukon. All of these actions were taken without consultation with any other province. In fact, some historians allege that Ottawa was most anxious not to consult the provinces when Newfoundland was admitted because there was a fear that Quebec would block the admission over its dispute with Newfoundland over the Quebec/Labrador boundary.

Under Canada's current constitution, however, the creation of new provinces not only requires federal consent but also the consent of seven provinces having at least 50 percent of

Canada's population. In practical terms, therefore, either Ontario or Quebec must be included among the seven. This requirement of provincial consent may prove to be a major hurdle for Nunavut. Nor does the constitution allow any mechanism whereby a northern territory may initiate provincehood. By contrast, section 146 of the British North America Act allowed for the admission of Newfoundland, Prince Edward Island and British Columbia into Confederation only after their legislatures had spoken in favour of joining Canada.

The failed Meech Lake Accord would have introduced even more stringent requirements. Under the accord, the consent of all ten provinces would have been required for the creation of new provinces. Arguing against the Meech Lake Accord, Yukon government leader Tony Penikett wrote:

> Regions of the country that have little connection to the reality of life in the north, or its state of political and economical development, will have a veto over its constitutional future. Were the economy to expand and the population of the Yukon to grow to several million, tiny Prince Edward Island would still be able to control our constitutional destiny.... Ironically, neither the Yukon nor the Northwest Territories would be present at the constitutional meetings to hear their own application for provincehood.

In both the United States and Australia new states can be admitted to the union without the requirement of consent from other states.

So why the change to make it harder to create a new province? Howard McConnell offers this speculation:

> Probably the desire to give Quebec a veto over such admissions figured prominently in the decision. Quebec, which is a guardian in the federation of what the Accord describes as a "distinct society," is already outnumbered by nine provinces with English-speaking majorities in the councils of Canadian executive federalism, and the addition of two more non-Francophone northern provinces would create an even greater imbalance.

Both the 1982 constitution and the Meech Lake Accord also dealt with the northward expansion of the provinces. The consent requirement for the northward extension of provinces was the same as needed to create new provinces. Northward expansion of the provinces is a very real issue, and it has surfaced from time to time, most recently in 1964.

The requirement of provincial consent for the creation of Nunavut is further complicated by the fact that Quebec announced, on the heels of the failure of the Meech Lake Accord, that it would take part in no further constitutional talks. The likelihood of a new province in those circumstances is indeed bleak.

There may also be a financial hurdle to overcome, as well, before Nunavut or other territories can become provinces. At the heart of the problem is the constitutionally entrenched equalization scheme. According to Gordon Robertson, a former commissioner of the NWT and clerk of the Privy Council, the provinces are likely to object that new provinces formed from the territories would require special financial treatment. In his study for the Institute for Research on Public Policy, *Northern Provinces: A Mistaken Goal*, Robertson points out that the tax yield in the NWT is greater than the national average, therefore disqualifying future northern provinces from receiving equalization payments. Such payments are based on per capita tax yield. However, because of the high cost of governing a small population in a large territory, with high costs of transportation and goods, the tax yield is not sufficient to support the government. Massive financial support from Ottawa is required. Robertson argues that it is unlikely that the provinces would agree to an equalization formula which would treat northern provinces such as Nunavut more favourably than other provinces.

There are counter-arguments. Section 36 of the constitution sets out the equalization scheme and states that Parliament and the provinces are committed to "promoting equal opportunities ...; furthering economic development to reduce disparity in opportunities; and providing essential services of reasonable quality to all Canadians." Subsection 2 then commits the federal government to making equalization payments to ensure that provincial governments have "sufficient revenues to provide reasonably comparable levels of public services at reasonably comparable levels of taxation." In other words, the method of calculating the formula is not enshrined in the constitution, only the concept of equal levels of public service at comparable taxation levels. The level of support could vary from province to province; section 36 does not preclude a province entering into special arrangements with Ottawa.

The Inuit argue that financial arrangements have varied as new provinces were admitted into Confederation and that economic self-sufficiency should not be the test for self-government. British Columbia came into Confederation on the promise of a railway. In a recent lawsuit in Federal Court, lawyers for PEI argued against a federal decision to close down all railways in the island: as part of the terms of union in 1873 the federal government had agreed to take over the railway. When Newfoundland joined Confederation, the terms of union deliberately left out mention of responsibility for Indian and Inuit people. And when Alberta, Manitoba and Saskatchewan became provinces, control over public lands and resources remained in federal hands. In short, the Inuit argue that these precedents simply mean that there are no hard and fast standards to be met for the creation of new provinces or territories and that special arrangements are possible. In the case of Nunavut, those special arrangements would include extra financial support.

There is validity to their argument. If economic self-sufficiency were the test of provincehood, a great many provinces might be giving up their provincial status. In the fiscal year ending in March 1991, seven of Canada's ten provinces received equalization payments totalling $8.3 billion from the federal government.

Provincehood also raises the population question. Is a province of 40,000 (the estimated population of the eastern Arctic in the year 2000) a viable province? In response, it should be borne in mind that population has never before been a criterion for provincehood. And there are precedents for the creation of provinces with small populations. With its 12,000 inhabitants, Manitoba formed less than 0.4 percent of Canada's 1870 population. And today Prince Edward Island represents less than 0.5 percent of Canada's population.

Suggested Alternatives to Nunavut

One alternative to the creation of Nunavut is to leave the territory as it is. There is a belief in some circles that as the Inuit of the eastern Arctic gain more prominence in territorial politics and a greater sense of their own power in the government, the idea of forming their own territory will fade. Proponents of the status quo point to how the political scene has changed since the concept of Nunavut was first proposed. The east has equal representation in the Assembly. Cabinet posts are divided between east and west, and a tradition has evolved that the position of government leader alternates between an easterner and a westerner. Inuktitut has become an official language. And if the land claims agreement is finalized the Inuit will have a greater say in wildlife management, land use and resource development in the eastern Arctic. There are many similarities in this approach to that adopted by Prime Minister Trudeau in proposing to Quebeckers that they really had a say in Ottawa and could be significant force nationally.

A different alternative to division, suggested by Gurston Dacks, is "consociation." Under this model there would be a central territorial government composed of councils representing each of the north's ethnic communities. Each council would have power over education, language, social policy, health and justice, and such other powers as defined in a new NWT charter. Each council would also be guaranteed a certain number of seats in the Assembly and in cabinet (or the executive council, as it is now known).

The problem with this model is that it would impose yet another level of government on an already over-governed territory. If this proposal were to become reality, NWT residents would be governed by four different levels: local municipal government (hamlet, village or town), regional council, territorial government and federal government. Most other Canadians are governed by only three levels.

As an alternative to provincehood, Gordon Robertson suggests the creation, by federal and territorial legislation, of autonomous federal territories having full self-governing powers. He believes that the constitution could be amended to approve such entities. This option was also mentioned in the 1988 territorial government discussion paper on political and constitutional development. It raises a number of serious questions. Would an autonomous government be that much different from a province? Would Canada's provinces be willing to accept that Canadian federalism could include this form of government? More important, would northern residents be willing to accept a government which in some ways would be perceived to be something less than full provincial government? This government would be the creation of federal legislation, with no constitutional protection for its powers. In essence, it would perpetuate the status quo, with the territorial government exercising many province-like powers.

If such an autonomous territory were created, could Ottawa proceed unilaterally to divide it and create new territories that might seek provincehood at some future time? Ottawa could devolve its powers to each of the newly created territories much as it is currently doing.

In essence, this option would involve sneaking in provincehood for Nunavut. The question is whether any province might object to a division of the territory and the devolution of province-like powers to its parts. It would seem that Ottawa has the constitutional power to do so. The only objection that a province could raise is that the new jurisdiction will undoubtedly not be happy with such status forever and will eventually seek provincehood.

6

Nunavut and Aboriginal Rights

The summer of 1990 will long be remembered by Canadians as the time when Canada's Aboriginal people, most notably the Indian nations, seized Canada's political agenda and put Aboriginal issues at the top. In the week before the deadline for the Meech Lake Accord's approval, Elijah Harper, the Manitoba MLA for the New Democratic Party representing Rupertsland, held up its passage in the Manitoba Legislature as the government tried to ram it through. He refused the unanimous consent needed to have the accord introduced without prior notice. His actions, coupled with those of Newfoundland Premier Clyde Wells, killed the Meech Lake Accord.

Three weeks after Harper's stand, in the early hours of July 10, one hundred heavily armed Quebec provincial police officers stormed a barricade erected by Mohawk Warriors on disputed land at Kanesatake (Oka), Quebec. That raid, against barricades which had been in place for four months, led to the death of a police officer and an armed standoff. The Mohawks of Kahnawake, south of Montreal, blocked off roads leading to the Mercier Bridge (which links south-shore communities to Montreal) in support of their kin at Kanesatake. The army had to be called in. The armed standoff lasted seventy-seven days.

Throughout this summer of discontent, the Inuit and their organizations remained largely silent. Only months before, they had signed an agreement-in-principle dealing with their land claim, and some progress was being made on their goal of Nunavut. But their silence did not mean that the Inuit were acquiescing in federal actions.

While there is often pessimism about the prospect for recognition of Aboriginal rights and claims, significant progress has been made since the 1970s. After prodding from the courts, the federal government altered its position on Aboriginal rights in 1973, and this has allowed the Inuit to advance their land claim successfully. And constitutional protection for treaty and Aboriginal rights has been achieved; the Inuit land claims agreement will be enforceable by Canada's highest law.

The Inuit Situation and the Indian/Métis Situation

While the Inuit sought to attain many of the same goals as their Aboriginal counterparts, the Inuit came to the negotiating table with a very different perspective and history than the Indian and Métis people.

No reserves were ever created for the Inuit, as there had been for the Indian people. Nor had promises been made to the Inuit, as there had been to the Indian people by way of treaty, or to the Métis by the way of the Manitoba Act and the Dominion Lands Act.

Treaties were used by the British, and later the federal government, as a means of acquiring the Aboriginal interest in land. (Today, we speak of "Aboriginal title" to land.) The treaties entered into with the Indians of the Maritimes had been treaties of peace and friendship, but after the Royal Proclamation of 1763, the Crown began to see treaties as a way of acquiring the Indian land interest. In that proclamation, George III promised to Indians all unsettled land as their hunting grounds, and further stated that lands required for settlement had to be acquired by the government from the Indians at a meeting attended by Indians for that purpose. (The territory covered by the proclamation has been a source of considerable debate among legal scholars.) Following that proclamation, treaties were entered into in what is today Ontario and the Prairie provinces. Treaty making continued until 1923, but few treaties were entered into in British Columbia or the north. Hence the modern-day land claim in those areas.

Métis claims for land on the prairies were dealt with by the Manitoba Act—which promised 1.4 million acres (about 570,000 hectares) and title to riverlots occupied by Métis—and the Dominion Lands Act, which offered the Métis scrip. Today, the Métis allege that because of government duplicity they never received the full benefit of those promises.

Consideration was first given to including the Inuit under a treaty in the 1920s. In August 1920, Imperial Oil struck oil at Norman Wells, halfway up the Mackenzie River. The prospect of extensive resource development in the area prompted the Superintendent General of Indian Affairs to urge the Minister of the Interior to enter into a treaty with the Dene Indians along the Mackenzie River. As at other times when development was about to proceed, no one wanted the Indians to be a hindrance to progress. So treaty inspector Henry Anthony Conroy was ordered to negotiate a treaty with the Indians who lived along the Mackenzie River from the 60th parallel to the Arctic Ocean. His efforts led to Treaty Number 11, which was signed in 1921 and 1922. Seven years later Governor General Byng and O. S. Finnie, director of the NWT Branch of the Department of the Interior, travelled to the Mackenzie Delta and met with the local Inuit in Aklavik. When asked if they wanted to join Treaty Number 11, the Inuit made clear they had no desire to do so.

Aside from this one offer to the Inuit to sign a treaty, no other discussion over the surrender of Aboriginal title was held with the Inuit until the modern land claims process began in the 1970s. In part, this was because there was no pressure to develop the eastern Arctic.

Not only were the Inuit not placed on reserves or required to sign treaties, they were also not subject to the same long-lasting pressures to assimilate as were the Indians and Métis. For centuries, governments made a concerted effort to eradicate Indian culture. Among other things, the federal Indian Act and regulations outlawed Indian cultural ceremonies such as the potlatch in B.C. and the sundance on the Prairies, imposed an elected form of government over traditional Indian governments such as that of the Mohawk Indians and put in place a pass system for prairie Indians wanting to leave their reserves. The Inuit did not face the onslaught of federal legislation and bureaucracy until the 1950s. Even into the 1960s, the Inuit lived well away from the mainstream of Canadian society.

It is the contention of some observers that this difference in historical experience has led the Inuit to be more trusting of the government. Equally, it has led them, by and large, to reject militant action in favour of the negotiating table.

The Inuit of the eastern Arctic have had another advantage over Aboriginal people in other parts of the country in dealing with land claims. The federal government has retained control over land in the north, so unlike much of southern Canada land claims can be settled there without the involvement of a provincial government.

It may also be to their advantage that many Canadians have formed a romantic notion of the Inuit. As one Indian woman in Yellowknife put it, "southerners and even white northerners look at the Dene and Métis and say they're just like the Indians in the south, but they look at the Inuit and see them in this romantic light, overlooking the many problems that Inuit society has."

Political Activism of the 1960s and 70s

The 1960s and early 1970s saw the growth of political activism among Canada's Aboriginal people. There were demands for an end to racism, for recognition and settlement of Aboriginal claims and for constitutional recognition for Aboriginal people. That activism took on many forms. Political and cultural organizations arose. Some Indian and Métis groups even occupied federal buildings and blockaded bridges. Many Canadians looking southward at the violence resulting from the Afro-American struggle in the United States feared similar outbreaks in Canada.

The Inuit took no violent action, but organized politically. The Inuit Tapirisat of Canada (ITC) was formed in 1971. It grew out of a meeting of Inuit leaders in Coppermine followed by a meeting in Toronto. The founding conference was held at Carleton University in Ottawa, with thirty delegates from the four regions of the NWT in which the Inuit lived—the western Arctic, Kitikmeot, Keewatin and Baffin—along with Inuit from Quebec and Labrador. The organization was the beneficiary of a federal policy announced several years earlier to provide core funding to Native organizations, and in its first year the ITC received $132,000 from the federal Secretary of State. The ITC was soon to become the most important vehicle for the advancement of the Inuit claim to Nunavut. In fact, one of the first orders of business for the new organization was to prepare their 1976 proposal, *Nunavut*.

Legal Developments, 1973–1991

A turning point in Native-white relations was the federal government's 1969 White Paper on Indian Policy. Introduced by Jean Chrétien, then Minister of Indian Affairs, the controversial paper proposed doing away with special status for Indians, doing away with treaties and turning over responsibility for Indians to the provinces. Turning to Aboriginal rights, the paper stated: "These are so general and undefined that it is not realistic to think of them as specific claims capable of remedy." Federal denial of Aboriginal rights would have had a severe impact on the Inuit. If there were no such thing as Aboriginal title in Canadian law, the Inuit would have no legal basis for advancing a land claim.

But the wheels of justice were going in a different direction. The Nishga Indians of northwestern B.C. sued for a declaration that they had Aboriginal title to some 2,500 square kilometres of land. While the Nishga lost, the Supreme Court of Canada established an important legal principle. Six of the seven judges hearing the case ruled that in law there was such a thing as Aboriginal title.

At the same time, the Inuit and Cree of northern Quebec were involved in a classic confrontation with the Quebec government over the massive James Bay hydroelectric development. While the Quebec government had undertaken to its federal counterpart to settle Native land claims when the boundary of Quebec was extended northward (including the area covered by the James Bay project) in 1912, development on the project proceeded as if the promise had never been made.

The Inuit and Cree of northern Quebec organized.

Somebody told us that there was a good legal argument we could use—called land claims—and we should put an injunction on this massive project ... use the land claims argument—aboriginal rights. Nobody in the North ever heard of this. Aboriginal rights was something completely new, it was something that the lawyers introduced to us ... It was a tool, not of our invention, but it was something that had a crack we could slide through.

This is how Inuit leader Mark Gordon recalled it at a 1987 constitutional conference sponsored by the Canadian Arctic Resources Committee.

In the early 1970s, Zebedee Nungak and Charlie Watt worked to organize the Northern Quebec Inuit Association. In December 1972 that association, along with the Grand Council of the Cree led by Billy Diamond, went to court seeking an injunction to stop the project until the rights of the Cree and Inuit were determined. Almost a year after the hearing had begun Mr. Justice Malouf ruled that the Indian and Inuit people had Aboriginal rights and ordered a halt to all work on the James Bay project. The decision was quickly appealed: both the Quebec Court of Appeal and the Supreme Court of Canada ruled that the injunction should be lifted. Both courts ruled only on the specific circumstances of the project, however; neither court dealt squarely with the issue of Aboriginal rights. It was because of this legal uncertainty as to the Quebec government's position that Premier Robert Bourassa decided to negotiate rather than risk further adverse judgments. The Native parties, unsure of the results of a protracted legal battle and concerned that the project would be completed before a final judgment was handed down, accepted the offer to negotiate. A final agreement was reached in November 1975.

At the same time, Judge Morrow of the NWT Supreme Court allowed the Dene to file a claim by way of caveat to a portion of the NWT. Not only did he allow the Dene to file this claim on the basis of Aboriginal title, but he went on to rule that treaties 8 and 11, which covered that area, did not have the effect of extinguishing Aboriginal rights because the signatory chiefs did not understand the terms of the treaty or agree to them. Morrow's decision forced the federal government to continue negotiations with the Dene.

Six years after Morrow's decision, in 1979, the Inuit of Baker Lake in the central NWT, backed by the ITC, were in Federal Court seeking a declaration that some 78,000 square kilometres in the Baker Lake area belonged to them. They also asked for a court order that no further mining permits be issued by the territorial or federal government in the uranium-rich area and that companies carrying out prospecting work be ordered to stop. The Inuit complained that the helicopters and prospecting camps were scaring away the caribou. Adding to the tensions in the area was a conflict between local residents and wildlife officers supported by the RCMP.

It was such tensions, fears and distrust of government that took the Inuit to court. This was the first and only time that the Inuit of the NWT sued for Aboriginal title. There were weeks of hearings, including hearings held in Baker Lake. A number of Inuit elders testified (in Inuktitut) that they could identify their traditional hunting grounds by the position and colour of Inukshuks (rock piles made into the likeness of a man, with arms, legs and a head) and would look at where the arm on an Inukshuk was pointing to determine the extent of their territory.

After hearing the evidence, Federal Court Judge Mahoney set out four criteria that had to be met to prove Aboriginal title. Those were, first, that the Inuit and their ancestors were members of an organized society; second, that this organized society occupied the specific territory claimed as Aboriginal lands; third, that all other organized societies were excluded; and finally, that the occupation was a fact at the time England asserted sovereignty. Judge Mahoney found that the Inuit met these conditions and declared that the Inuit title existed in the lands surrounding Baker Lake. He refused, however, to stop prospecting activity, ruling that while the caribou herd had declined, mining exploration was not a significant factor in the decline, and further holding that federal and territorial mining legislation could abrogate Aboriginal title.

While Quebec Justice Malouf's judgment had forced the parties to the negotiating table, no such thing happened after Mahoney's judgment. Simply put, his decision placed no development project in jeopardy which would have forced the government to negotiate. Nor was Mahoney's judgment a total victory for the Inuit. While Mahoney granted a declaration in favour of the Inuit, he also held that the federal and territorial governments were within their rights to issue exploratory permits to the mining companies and could limit the scope of Aboriginal rights. Nevertheless, the case was an important legal milestone in the fight for Inuit rights. Not only did it recognize Inuit Aboriginal rights but it set out the criteria that had to be met to prove Aboriginal title. And in determining whether the Inuit were an organized society, Mahoney said that assessment should be made on the basis of local Inuit standards, not standards developed elsewhere.

In the midst of the very first rounds of court litigation, the federal government had retreated from its position of 1969. In August 1973, Jean Chrétien announced that the government would negotiate to settle Aboriginal land claims, and as part of the package announced the availability of funding, some of it by way of loan, for Native groups to document their cases. The government stated its willingness to deal with two kinds of claims: comprehensive claims for the surrender of Aboriginal title and specific claims arising from unfulfilled treaty obligations. In order to create finality and not to have to negotiate income sharing from Aboriginal lands on an ongoing basis, the government insisted that any land claim had to amount to a total surrender and extinguishment of the Aboriginal land right. An Office of Native Claims was established in 1974, but did not lead to the settlement of any claims.

Chrétien's 1973 policy was restated and refined in a 1981 document called *In All Fairness*, but it too achieved limited success. The only major claim settled under the new policy was the Inuvialuit Final Agreement. One impediment was that the government limited the number of claims it would negotiate at one time to six. An equal impediment was that in southern Canada provincial involvement was needed for the successful resolution of claims, because public lands there are owned by provincial governments.

The policy was reviewed and revised again at the end of 1986, following the recommendations of a federal task force headed by Murray Coolican. His study, *Living Treaties: Lasting Agreements*, concluded that at the rate claims were being settled "it could be another 100 years before all the claims have been addressed." Several major departures were made from earlier policies as a result of Coolican's recommendations. Under the old policy the government demanded extinguishment of Aboriginal title throughout the claims area and surrender of all Aboriginal rights in exchange for money, land set aside and other benefits. Under the new policy Aboriginal title could continue on those lands set aside for Native people. In a concession of particular importance to the Inuit, the government agreed to negotiate offshore rights including harvesting, management and sharing of resources. The government also indicated a readiness to share resource revenue with Aboriginal groups. And for northern claims, the government announced that the territorial governments would sit as part of the federal negotiating team.

Three major agreements-in-principle were signed on the basis of the new policy: the claim by the Council of Yukon Indians, the claim by the Dene/Métis of the NWT and the claim of the eastern Arctic Inuit.

The cause of Native claims was further advanced by the May 1990 Supreme Court of Canada decision in the Sparrow case. Ronald Sparrow from the Musqueam Indian Band in Vancouver was charged with fishing with a drift net longer than the 25 fathoms allowed under the Fisheries Act regulations. Sparrow's lawyers argued that his right to fish was an Aboriginal right protected by Canada's constitution, which recognizes and affirms the "existing aboriginal and treaty rights of the aboriginal peoples of Canada."

In its landmark ruling, the Supreme Court said that all Aboriginal rights remained in force unless there had been clear and unequivocal legislation to extinguish those rights. The Court went on to say that in spite of the protection in the constitution, governments could pass legislation restricting Aboriginal rights. The onus of showing that there was an interference with Aboriginal rights was on Aboriginal people themselves. In deciding whether there was interference a court had to look at whether the legislation imposed an undue hardship on Aboriginal people, whether it interfered with their preferred way of exercising their rights and whether there was a legitimate reason for the legislation. If there was interference, the burden was then on the government to show that the restriction was justified, that in passing the law the honour of the Crown in its dealings with Aboriginal people was maintained, that Aboriginal people had been consulted, that consideration was given to ensuring that the interference was minimal and that compensation was offered for rights taken away. If those tests were met, then the legislation would be valid. In the Sparrow case the Supreme Court ruled that conservation was a valid legislative objective and could take priority over Aboriginal rights. The court also went on to say that if a conservation scheme for fish or game was necessary any allocation of game resources must give first priority to Aboriginal food needs.

The Sparrow case has had significant ramifications for Aboriginal land claims. For many Aboriginal people the case represented an affirmation of the existence of Aboriginal rights. It led to a great many Dene and Métis people rethinking their position on the land claims agreement they had signed in April 1990. "For all we know we might be the owners of all the north," one Dene spokesperson said. "Why should we give away all our rights for a few parcels of land, some money and representation on some government boards?" It was that position that led the Dene to reject their final agreement in the summer of 1990.

There were also negative messages from the courts. Land claims from northwestern B.C. had returned to the courts in 1987 when the Gitksan Wet'suwet'en Tribal Council commenced an action for a declaration that they owned over 57,000 square kilometres of northwestern British Columbia. The decision was rendered in mid-March 1991. British Columbia Chief Justice McEachern ruled that while the Gitksan and Wet'suwet'en had some rights to the territory, their rights did not amount to ownership, and in any event their limited rights had been extinguished by the unilateral actions of the pre-Confederation B.C. colonial government. Many legal scholars have argued that the decision flies in the face of the Sparrow case, which required clear language for title to be extinguished. The case is expected to reach the Supreme Court of Canada.

The 1982 Constitution

Throughout the 1970s the Inuit, along with other Native people, came to the conclusion that constitutional change was needed to protect their culture and way of life, and to secure a land base and the right to self-government. Their views on the need for constitutional reform happened to coincide with Pierre Trudeau's belief that Canada needed a new constitution.

In 1976 Trudeau wrote to all the premiers inviting them to join in repatriating the constitution. Little came of this initiative, but it did allow the Trudeau government to show some openness to Native concerns in 1978, in proposing a Charter of Rights that would not override lands reserved as hunting grounds for Indian people in the Royal Proclamation of 1763.

Throughout 1978 and 1979 the three national Native groups—the National Indian Brotherhood (now known as the Assembly of First Nations), the Native Council of Canada and the Inuit Tapirisat—lobbied for additional constitutional protection. At the October 1978 first ministers' conference these groups were granted observer status, and at the next conference in February 1979 the first ministers agreed that future conferences would discuss Canada's Native people and the constitution.

At its 1979 annual meeting in Igloolik, the ITC formed a special body, the Inuit Committee on National Issues, to advance the Inuit case as Canada worked towards constitutional reform.

Native people won an important concession during Joe Clark's brief tenure as prime minister—they were allowed to speak at constitutional conferences. When Trudeau returned to power in February 1980 the constitution once again became one of the central issues of national politics. He announced that the federal government would make a unilateral request to the British Parliament to repatriate the constitution. Shortly afterwards the government submitted its constitutional resolution to Parliament. This resolution made provision for a Charter of Rights but offered no protection for Aboriginal rights. Trudeau attributed this omission to the difficulty of defining Aboriginal rights.

By the fall of 1980, Native groups had succeeded in obtaining public support for their efforts to entrench Aboriginal rights in the constitution. The Canadian Bar Association, the Robarts-Pepin Task Force on National Unity, the Joint Senate–House of Commons Committee on the Constitution, the Primate of the Anglican Church, the Ontario Conference of Catholic Bishops, and others, all called for special provisions in the constitution protecting Native rights. After the Trudeau government introduced its resolution in October 1980, the lobbying campaign achieved even greater intensity. Native groups besieged the Canadian and British parliaments as well as the United Nations, urging those bodies to lend their weight in pressuring the Canadian government to protect Native rights in the constitution.

The lobbying worked. On January 30, 1981, Jean Chrétien, then Justice Minister, introduced an amendment to the proposed constitution that "recognized and affirmed" the "aboriginal and treaty rights" of Canada's Aboriginal people. The term "Aboriginal people" was defined to include Indian, Inuit and Métis people. The amendment also promised that a conference to define Aboriginal rights would be held within two years, with Aboriginal participants.

But Ottawa's package was watered down in order to gain provincial support. So the draft constitution agreed on in November 1981 by Ottawa and all provinces except Quebec omitted all protection for Aboriginal and treaty rights because some provinces opposed such recognition. This produced an immediate public backlash from both Native and non-Native groups.

Within weeks, the first ministers changed their position. Alberta Premier Peter Lougheed was the last holdout; he agreed to include Aboriginal rights in the draft constitution if the word "existing" was added. Section 35 of the constitution now read, "The existing aboriginal and treaty rights of the aboriginal peoples of Canada are hereby recognized and affirmed."

The word "existing" was a red flag to Aboriginal leaders. As they saw it, the word meant that only those rights existing when the constitution came into force would be protected, and that future rights such as self-government could gain no protection. They feared that rights that Native people had once enjoyed, but had been taken away before 1982, would not be protected.

The Constitutional Conferences of 1983 to 1987

The new constitution required that a conference be held within one year of its coming into force, to identify and define Aboriginal rights. That conference was held on March 15 and 16, 1983. Another three conferences followed between 1984 and 1987. The 1983 conference was the only one that achieved significant progress.

The parties to the 1983 conference agreed that no constitutional changes affecting Aboriginal rights would be made without a constitutional conference to which Aboriginal people were invited. (This did not go as far as some Aboriginal leaders had hoped—that is, an absolute veto over constitutional changes affecting them.) With this in mind, they planned on holding three more constitutional conferences by April 1987. The agenda of the next conference would include self-government, equality rights, treaties, Aboriginal title and rights, and land and resources.

Two other items were agreed upon. The constitutional guarantee for existing treaty and Aboriginal rights was extended to include future land claims agreements—a significant provision for the Inuit, as it would mean that their land claims would be constitutionally protected. Finally, the constitution was amended to guarantee sexual equality in the area of constitutionally protected Aboriginal and treaty rights. The sexual equality amendment created some difficulty.

Follow-up conferences were held on March 8 and 9, 1984, and April 2 and 3, 1985. At both conferences, far too much time was spent trying to come up with a better sexual equality section. Aboriginal leaders accused the government of changing the equality section without consent.

The other major issue discussed at the two conferences was self-government. Although the Liberal government had been replaced by a Conservative one by the time of the 1985 conference, the federal proposals on self-government were remarkably similar at both conferences. These proposals recognized the right of Aboriginal people to self-governing institutions and stated that the jurisdiction, powers and financing of those institutions were to be negotiated with the provinces and federal government.

At the 1984 conference, the federal proposal for self-government was strongly supported by Manitoba, Ontario and New Brunswick but foundered on the opposition of B.C., Alberta and Saskatchewan, and also of the Native groups. The main concern of the Native groups was that only the negotiation process was constitutionally protected, but that there was no guarantee of protection for the results it achieved. They also feared that the negotiations on institutions of self-government might never take place or might end in stalemate.

The 1985 conference took off where the 1984 one had finished. There were great expectations for the talks—Brian Mulroney, the great labour conciliator, was in the chair. On the first day of the conference, Saskatchewan, Alberta and B.C. refused to include a statement in the constitution recognizing self-government until that principle was defined. On the second day, Saskatchewan tried to break the impasse by proposing an amendment in which constitutional recognition of self-government was contingent upon negotiation. It was accepted by six other provinces and the federal government; Alberta and British Columbia opposed it and Quebec, which refused to recognize the 1982 constitution, abstained. Although there were sufficient votes to pass the amendment, the prime minister wanted the support of the Aboriginal organizations. The Métis National Council and the Native Council of Canada decided to support the Saskatchewan formula after Mulroney agreed that he would meet with them to discuss a land base for the Métis and non-status Indians. The Assembly of First Nations, however, rejected the Saskatchewan proposal because it contained no commitment that negotiations implementing the principle of self-government would be undertaken. The Inuit Committee on National Issues withheld their judgment for further consultation with their people.

The prime minister adjourned the conference until June 5 and 6, 1985, for senior cabinet ministers from all governments and Aboriginal leaders to continue discussions and to await the Inuit answer. That meeting came to nothing.

Of the four constitutional conferences on Aboriginal rights, the 1987 conference was the greatest disaster. Unlike previous conferences, the whole of the first day was taken up with opening statements. There was no negotiation. Many participants left the impression that they were simply putting in time to fulfil the constitutional requirement that another conference be held. All parties stressed the need for Aboriginal people to have greater control over their daily affairs, but they could not agree on what words should be put in the constitution.

The Aboriginal leaders had all agreed beforehand on a common position—that self-government was an inherent right and that its implementation would be subject to negotiations in "good faith." Their proposal required governments to enter into self-government negotiations; it affirmed the inherent right of the Indian, Inuit and Métis people to a land base; and it gave Aboriginal people the right, if they so chose, to call for treaty renegotiations. The Aboriginal parties did not move from their position during the two-day conference.

The conference ended in recriminations. Prime Minister Mulroney showed annoyance with some of the western provinces: "We had seven provinces on side in 1985 ... some people have started to go backwards."

John Amagoalik, co-chair of the Inuit Committee on National Issues, declared: "I say to the aboriginal peoples of the Northwest Territories, from which I come, because this conference has failed we must work even harder to create Nunavut and Denendeh. We cannot allow anyone to steal that from us." Native leaders were left with the fear that, without constitutional protection, their rights could be taken away at will by the government.

After $50 million and five years, the constitutional process ended without concrete results. On the positive side, the process gave Native issues a public profile they had not had before, while also providing Native leaders with political experience at the national level. On the negative side, hopes which had been raised in 1982 were brutally smashed; ultimately, this led to Aboriginal leaders venting their anger as the Manitoba Legislature struggled with a last-ditch attempt to save the Meech Lake Accord in June 1990.

The Meech Lake Accord

A month after the failed Aboriginal constitutional conference of 1987, Canada's first ministers reached an agreement to amend the constitution to satisfy Quebec's aspirations. After the tedious negotiations on Aboriginal rights, most Canadians were stunned at the speed with which these negotiations proceeded. On June 3, thirty-five days after the agreement-in-principle had been reached, Canada's first ministers produced the actual wording for the amended constitution. It recognized Quebec as a distinct society and allowed the provinces a say in immigration and in appointments to the Supreme Court of Canada and the Senate. Provinces were given the right to opt out of national social programs and receive compensation from Ottawa in return. The requirements to amend the constitution were also changed. Unanimous provincial consent was required for changes to the Senate and the role of the Queen, governor general and lieutenant-governors, and for the creation of new provinces.

To the Dene, Métis and Inuit of the Northwest Territories, the latter requirement was a major setback. Given the Meech Lake Accord's more onerous requirement for the creation of new provinces, the Inuit dream of Nunavut and maybe a future province suddenly seemed so much farther away. All residents of the Territories and of the Yukon feared that the new provisions would prevent them from having a say in appointments to the Senate and Supreme Court of Canada, a privilege reserved for the provinces.

The accord made only passing reference to Canada's Aboriginal people. It stated that recognizing Quebec as a distinct society would not affect any rights Native people already have under the constitution.

The accord received the approval of Parliament and eight provinces. An all-party parliamentary committee studied the accord on two occasions. In the first study, it called on the federal government to continue to fund Native groups preparing their constitutional case. It also called for a first ministers' conference on Aboriginal rights to be held by April 17, 1990— which, of course, was never held.

The committee made a number of recommendations concerning the north. It supported the right of the Yukon and NWT to present names for appointments to the Supreme Court of Canada and called for clarification on the right of the territories to name senators. But on the difficult question of political development in the north, the committee simply called for more study. There was no mention of division of the NWT or the creation of Nunavut. This prompted Nunatsiaq MP Thomas Suluk, in an October 1987 Commons speech, to say: "I do not understand why the specific joint committee does not mention Nunavut. Perhaps they did not listen to the Inuit."

But Suluk didn't need to worry about the accord. As its June 23, 1990, deadline approached it became clear that it was facing major opposition, even in provinces that initially had signed it. Changes in provincial governments had led to its reconsideration in Manitoba, New Brunswick and Newfoundland. Opponents of the accord—Aboriginal people, women and people who feared a shift of power from the federal to the provincial level—focused their lobbying efforts on those provinces.

A parliamentary committee again studied the accord to try to break the deadlock. In its May 1990 report the committee recommended further constitutional talks on Aboriginal issues and that the requirement of unanimous consent for the creation of new provinces be dropped. But Robert Bourassa rejected the committee report because, among other things, it asked for a companion resolution that the accord's distinct society clause does not in any way impair the Charter of Rights and Freedoms.

After a week-long first ministers' meeting in early June designed to save the accord, an agreement was reached for the holdout provinces to put the accord to a vote by its June 23 deadline. The first ministers promised that a constitutional conference on Aboriginal rights would be held every three years, and that the requirements for creation of a new province would be the subject of a future constitutional conference.

In mid-June the three holdout provinces put the accord to a vote in their legislatures. New Brunswick approved. Clyde Wells put it before the Newfoundland Assembly, but withdrew it on the day before the deadline, pending the outcome in Manitoba. It was in Manitoba that events played out most dramatically. Elijah Harper, who had undertaken the role of Aboriginal voice on the accord, delayed its introduction in the Manitoba Legislature for nearly a week. Once introduced, he succeeded in using procedural tactics to delay its progress through the legislature. Harper received strong support from Aboriginal groups throughout Canada who held public demonstrations in various Canadian centres. Meanwhile, in a letter to Phil Fontaine, leader of the Assembly of Manitoba Chiefs, Brian Mulroney appealed for co-operation in passing the accord, pointing out the progress that had been made on Aboriginal rights and promising a "major Royal Commission on Native Affairs." But finally, on the day before the accord's deadline, Harper spoke for hours in the legislature, refusing to give the unanimous consent needed for the bill to come to a vote.

With the death of the accord, Quebec Premier Robert Bourassa declared that his government would no longer participate in federal-provincial conferences. In his words, "there is no question of discussing constitutional reform that could include the Native people."

There were many irritants in the Meech Lake Accord for Aboriginal people. Perhaps what rankled the most was the recognition of the English- and French-speaking societies as fundamental characteristics of Canada and of Quebec as a distinct society. Aboriginal people argued that they were as distinct as Quebec society. And to arguments of Quebec's future being threatened they pointed out that their societies were in even greater jeopardy. Of Canada's fifty-three Aboriginal languages only three, Cree, Ojibway and Inuktitut, are showing the strength to survive. *The Globe and Mail* has identified ten of these languages as being near extinction or in danger.

Aboriginal Rights After the Summer of 1990

On the heels of the failed Meech Lake Accord, frustrations in the Native community, particularly among Indians and Métis, boiled over. The flashpoint was Oka, followed by a series of blockades across the country.

Then a number of positive announcements were made. British Columbia, in a surprise policy announcement, agreed to sit down at the bargaining table to settle land claims. Saskatchewan agreed to deal with unfulfilled treaty promises. Treaty commissioner Cliff Wright came up with a cash-for-land formula as a proposal for settling outstanding treaty land entitlement in that province. His report led to negotiations between the Federation of Saskatchewan Indian Nations and the federal and provincial governments, with a tentative agreement reached in the spring of 1992.

There were other surprising developments. At an August 1990 meeting of provincial premiers in Winnipeg, six premiers called for further constitutional talks (excluding talks on self-government, however) with Aboriginal people. A new Ontario government, led by NDP Premier Bob Rae, promised that it would do its part to help establish Aboriginal self-government and eventually announced its recognition of the inherent right of Aboriginal people to self-government. (That is to say, it is a right that has always existed and is not dependent on the government's granting it.) At the same time, Indian Affairs Minister Thomas Siddon undertook to settle all outstanding

Native claims. In September 1990, Prime Minister Mulroney announced his new agenda for dealing with Aboriginal peoples. Among other things he announced a speeded up process to settle land claims; the federal government would no longer restrict itself to negotiating no more than six comprehensive claims at one time. Several months later, in the spring of 1991, Mulroney announced the formation of a royal commission to examine Aboriginal issues. In a departure from tradition, the prime minister first asked retired Supreme Court Chief Justice Brian Dickson to advise him on the scope of the commission and on possible appointees to it. Four of its seven members are Aboriginal people, including an Inuk woman. At the time of writing it was just beginning its work.

And in the ongoing constitutional renewal process, in early July 1991 Constitutional Affairs Minister Joe Clark announced that Native people would be allowed to have and run their own constitutional assembly to define their position and role within the Canadian federation.

Later that year, the federal government came up with a new constitutional package. Under that proposal the federal government promised to recognize the Aboriginal right to self-government and to place that right in the constitution. That right was to become enforceable in ten years; in the meantime, governments were to undertake to negotiate implementation of that right. There would be regular first ministers' conferences on the subject.

The proposal caused concern among many Aboriginal peoples. Why, they asked, was Quebec immediately being recognized as a distinct society while their right to self-government was being delayed for ten years? They demanded constitutional recognition as distinct societies in their own right. They also pressed for recognition that their right to self-government was an inherent right. And they argued for another first ministers' conference on Aboriginal issues.

The Grand Chief of the Assembly of First Nations, Ovide Mercredi, took his battle to a committee of Quebec's National Assembly considering sovereignty. He argued, as he had before, that the First Nations are as distinct as Quebeckers. He denied that Quebec could speak for its Aboriginal people and make decisions for them.

Late in 1991, the federal government sponsored a series of five mini-constitutional conferences to which a wide spectrum of the Canadian public was invited. At the end of the series, in mid-February 1992, there seemed to be public support for the entrenchment in the constitution of the inherent right to self-government for Aboriginal people. The consensus seemed to be that such a right should be limited and should be subject to the Charter of Rights and Freedoms.

A final constitutional conference in the series was held in early March. It focused on Aboriginal issues and not only wholeheartedly approved of constitutionalizing an inherent right to self-government, but also confirmed that Aboriginal peoples should have a voice in other constitutional meetings (something which occurred in the ongoing talks in spring 1992). Later, there appeared to be some consensus among provincial governments that a right of self-government could be described in the constitution, without being defined. So optimistic was Constitutional Affairs Minister Joe Clark after one May meeting of provincial officials that he described the process as an agreement to create a third order of government. At the time of writing that third order of government still needed approval from Canada's first ministers, and of course the approval of the federal Parliament and at least seven provincial legislatures representing 50 percent of Canada's population in order to become a part of the constitution. In early June 1992, the issue of Senate reform yet threatened to jeopardize any agreement. There were other developments. Ovide Mercredi, the AFN chief, and Quebec Premier Robert Bourassa agreed to meet regularly to discuss Aboriginal issues. And there was even speculation that Quebec might return to the constitutional bargaining table.

Perhaps the brightest spot in Canada's struggle to achieve an accommodation with Aboriginal people was the work that was proceeding towards the creation of Nunavut.

Nunavut is being built on the struggle of Aboriginal people for recognition of their rights. It was the recognition of Aboriginal land rights that led the federal government and the Inuit to a land claims agreement. That land claims agreement—if ratified—will be protected under the constitution, thanks to the lobbying efforts and lengthy negotiations undertaken in the name of all Canada's Aboriginal peoples.

Two demands relating to Aboriginal land rights remain outstanding. Those are the claims for further constitutional recognition for their land rights and distinct status, and the right to further recognition for self-government. It is here that Nunavut may represent a substantial breakthrough for Aboriginal people. Given current prospects, Nunavut may well be the first Aboriginal government to have provincial-type powers. And as such it may be the answer to those critics who fear that an Aboriginal government may not work. Nunavut may well represent the first genuine power sharing with Aboriginal people. Its creation will serve as an example of what other Aboriginal peoples can achieve. It is important to understand that the quest for Nunavut is part of the larger struggle by Aboriginal people for justice and self-government.

7

Inuit Land Claims

"I'm surprised we still have a language ... Our culture has really taken a beating, we don't have drum dancing or traditional cultural activities of other Inuit communities...," William Andersen, president of the Labrador Inuit Association, said in a 1990 *Globe and Mail* interview.

When Canadians think about the Inuit, the focus is on the eastern Arctic and the Mackenzie Delta area, but it should be borne in mind that there are also significant Inuit populations in Quebec and Labrador.

The Inuit of Labrador

According to archaeologist Robert McGhee in *Canadian Arctic Prehistory*, the Arctic Small Tool people, the pre-Dorsets and the Dorsets all occupied Labrador. And, according to McGhee, between 500 B.C. and A.D. 500 the Dorsets were the most numerous and perhaps the only Aboriginal people in Newfoundland. The Thule people, the predecessors of the modern-day Inuit, are believed to have moved into Labrador around the year 1500, when they crossed Hudson Strait and came as far south as Hamilton Inlet. There are indications that they occupied not only the coast of Labrador but also parts of Newfoundland and parts of the Quebec coast south of Labrador to the Gulf of St. Lawrence.

A state of war existed between the Inuit people and European explorers and fishermen during the fifteenth and sixteenth centuries. During the sixteenth and early seventeenth centuries the Inuit travelled to trade in the Strait of Belle Isle, and would occasionally raid a fishing station. The conflict ended in 1765, when, under the encouragement of Jens Haven, a Moravian missionary, the Inuit entered into a peace treaty with the English. The Moravian Brothers, a mostly German religious sect, were in Greenland as early as 1733. Their first attempt to gain a foothold in Labrador in 1752 failed when the ship's crew was murdered as they landed near Hopedale. This failure aroused the interest of one of the Brothers, Jens Haven, a Dane who was fluent in Inuktitut. He led another mission in 1764 which made successful contact with the Inuit. According to archival reports there was discussion about the Inuit selling the land. In a 1770 encounter near Cape Harrison one of the Brothers reportedly addressed the Inuit as follows: "Look, I have written your names down here. Now I want each of you to make a sign against it, with his own hand, to the best of his ability. This will be an everlasting token of the fact that you have sold the land to us."

Similar encounters were repeated at other centres. At the same time, the British government began making grants to the Moravians for their missions.

Today the land cessions by the Inuit to the Moravians, if in fact they were such, are not regarded as amounting to a surrender by the Inuit of their land rights. In 1763, in the Royal Proclamation, the British Crown made clear that Native land could be acquired only by the Crown, and that surrenders to private individuals would not be recognized. While the Proclamation may not have had effect in Labrador (legal scholars have had many debates as to its geographic limit), it enunciated the policy that the British planned to carry out (not always successfully) in their dealings with Canada's Aboriginal people.

The Moravians established a number of missions and trading posts; between 1770 and 1830 the posts at Nain, Okak, Hopedale and Hebron were founded. Schools were established at each centre: the Moravian Brothers have often been credited with bringing a high degree of literacy to the Inuit of Labrador. They were teaching in the Inuktitut language in Nain in 1791, and they printed a hymn book in Inuktitut in 1809. Unfortunately, with Confederation in 1949, Inuktitut was forbidden in the schools and replaced by English.

Today, most Labrador Inuit live in Nain, Hopedale and Makkovik. A number also live in Happy Valley and Northwest River. As a result of relocation policies in the 1950s there are now no Inuit north of Nain. The Innu, who gained prominence in recent years by trying to block the jet fighter activities at

Goose Bay, are not Inuit, but Montagnais Indians. The two groups, however, are neighbours and some of the territory claimed by the Inuit overlaps some of that claimed by the Innu.

The claim of the 3,500 Inuit of Labrador was accepted by the federal government for negotiation in 1978, and in 1980 the Newfoundland government agreed to participate in the negotiations, though a Newfoundland deputy minister admitted in 1988 that "Newfoundland is doing this reluctantly because of federal pressure and the threat of court action." The federal decision to negotiate came after a major study commissioned by the Labrador Inuit Association was published in 1977, titled *Our Footprints Are Everywhere: Inuit Land Use and Occupancy in Labrador.*

Negotiations were stalled until 1988 because the Newfoundland government insisted that first there should be a federal-provincial agreement on handling the claim. In 1990 the two governments signed a framework agreement outlining the scope, process, topics and parameters for negotiation. The area to which the Inuit claim Aboriginal title runs from Fish Cove in the south to Cape Chidley in the north, then south along the Labrador-Quebec border and then across to Lake Melville (just north of Happy Valley–Goose Bay). The Inuit have been actively involved in commercial fishing and as a result their claim includes a portion of the Labrador Sea as well. At the time of writing, negotiations on the claim were continuing.

The Inuvialuit Claim

As we have seen, some of the Inuvialuit living in the Mackenzie Delta area can trace their habitation of the area only to the early 1900s. Nevertheless, as petroleum development threatened to take over the Beaufort Sea area, the Inuvialuit decided to press their claim.

In the first instance their organization, the Committee for Original Peoples' Entitlement (COPE), threw in its hat with their eastern Arctic sisters. However, as resource development pressed in on the Beaufort Sea area and as the Nunavut proposal of the Inuit was withdrawn in 1977 for more community consultation, COPE decided to advance its own claim. It was prosposed to the federal government in 1977, under the title "Inuvialuit Nunangat." Because of the oil and gas exploration activity in the area the government was most anxious to reach an agreement; an agreement-in-principle was reached in 1978, with a final agreement signed on June 5, 1984. The 1984 land claim settlement with the Inuvialuit represented the first major land claim settlement under the federal land claims policy announced in 1973.

Under that agreement the 2,500 Inuvialuit surrendered all their rights to 344,000 square kilometres covering the western Arctic coast from the Yukon border to the centre of Victoria Island, then running north to the 80th parallel. Inuvik and Aklavik form the southern boundary of the settlement area. The community of Coppermine is not included. Under the agreement the Inuvialuit are given the responsibility of defining their own membership. Membership is open to anyone accepted by the community as Inuvialuit and anyone with at least one Inuvialuit grandparent who produces evidence that he or she was born in the area or has been resident in the area for at least ten years.

In return for surrendering their rights, the Inuvialuit were granted title to 91,000 square kilometres and mineral rights in one-seventh of that zone. The land that included mineral rights was divided into blocks, with one such block near each of the six communities included in the settlement area: Aklavik, Inuvik, Tuktoyaktuk, Paulatuk, Holman and Sachs Harbour, and a seventh block on Cape Bathurst. The land granted amounts to approximately 36 square kilometres per individual, of which approximately 5 square kilometres includes full mineral rights. The land received by the Inuvialuit amounts to approximately one-third to one-half of all the lands the Inuvialuit traditionally used.

According to Peter Cumming, an Osgoode Hall law professor who has acted as legal adviser to the Inuvialuit, "there will never be as comprehensive an agreement ever again and because of that there is some jealousy. There will be no other settlement like this because it's now perceived as being too generous. Other northerners look on with envy on this settlement, perhaps knowing that they'll never get anything like this."

Richard Bartlett, in his study *Indian Reserves and Aboriginal Lands in Canada: A Homeland*, concluded that the settlement was far more generous than the James Bay Agreement or any treaty. Under western Canadian treaties, which were the most generous of treaties signed, one square mile (2.59 square kilometres) was set aside for every family of five. Under the James Bay Agreement the Inuit received approximately half the land per person that the Inuvialuit did.

In addition, the Inuvialuit received $152 million compensation payable over a thirteen-year period, with the final payment of $32 million to be made in 1997.

A corporate structure was set up to represent the Inuvialuit interest. The parent Inuvialuit Regional Corporation (the successor to COPE) is controlled by the six communities, each of which has one share in the corporation. There are a number of subsidiary corporations. The Inuvialuit Land Corporation owns the land, which is, however, administered by the Inuvialuit Land Administration. According to Cumming, the IRC is probably the biggest landholder in Canada. The Inuvialuit Development Corporation was set up to receive some of the financial compensation and to carry on business. Most of the money has been invested in businesses or investments. However, some dividends have been paid out to members. In appreciation of their role in helping achieve the settlement, each elder fifty years and older was paid $2,500. In addition, elders also receive two payments per year of $500 each. The only other dividend paid out has been a one-time $100 payment to each member.

No shares in the Inuvialuit corporations may be sold to private third parties.

The business activities of the Inuvialuit Development Corporation include ownership of an airline company serving the western Arctic, a shipping company serving the Mackenzie River and western Arctic communities, and a variety of other interests. Its construction arm, Koblunaq Construction, is by far the most significant player in western Arctic construction. The Inuvialuit Investment Corporation is the subsidiary formed to receive funds from the settlement: it invests in securities. Income earned by the IRC from its lands or investments is taxable.

The petroleum corporation belonging to the Inuvialuit has established a tutorial program for students starting in grade 6. Teachers who are interested are paid a supplement to provide additional tutorial services. "The idea is to develop a cadre of managers; we want accountants, engineers," says Anne Matheson, an executive assistant at the Inuvialuit Regional Corporation. "What we really need is training," says Roger Gruben, the Regional Corporation's chairman.

The agreement also provided economic and social development benefits. The Inuvialuit were granted $10 million for an economic enhancement fund, a promise of a fair crack at government contracts and a $7.5 million social development fund to assist with housing, health and welfare, education and cultural support.

The Inuvialuit settlement has a number of other important provisions. The Inuvialuit are given a major role to play in screening development in the area. Before any project can proceed, including government projects, it must be screened by the Environmental Impact Screening Committee. The committee, composed equally of Inuvialuit and government representatives with a joint chair, decides whether a project requires assessment. The committee considers the need to preserve local culture and values, to ensure that Inuvialuit are meaningful participants in northern development, and to protect and preserve Arctic wildlife and the environment. If the committee finds against a development proposal it sends it to the Environmental Impact Review Board, which also has equal government and Inuvialuit representation, or to any other body that can ensure Inuvialuit participation, has the power to impose limits on liability for wildlife compensation and can get an expeditious response from the minister involved. The federal government cannot approve a project until the process is complete, and although it can overrule the decision, it must give reasons for doing so.

Perhaps the most significant decision the board has made in its short history was its 1990 decision calling on the Minister of Indian and Northern Affairs to reject a Gulf Resources proposal for a three-year drilling program in the Beaufort Sea. The board found that Gulf did not have an adequate plan for a worst-case scenario, a well blowout. Although the government was tardy in its response, creating the impression that it was not taking the agreement seriously, it eventually created a steering committee of government, industry and Inuvialuit representatives to address the issues raised by the board's report.

There are also wildlife provisions in the Inuvialuit agreement. Inuvialuit are given the exclusive right to hunt fur-bearing animals and musk-ox on Inuvialuit lands. They are to be given preference in hunting all wildlife, except for certain migratory birds. An Inuvialuit Game Council was made up of representatives from each of the hunter and trapper committees in the six communities. The council allocates quotas among the communities, advises the government on wildlife polices and appoints Inuvialuit representatives to joint committees. Hunters and trappers who suffer loss as a result of any development are entitled to compensation from the developer.

Unlike the James Bay Agreement and the agreement-in-principle with the Inuit of the eastern Arctic, there is no provision for local government. However, Peter Cumming believes that the Inuvialuit Regional Corporation "could be the focus for one." In an April 1990 interview, Roger Gruben said, "We would like to see the IRC develop into a regional government, but right now we're just supporting communities to get what they want as the territorial government devolves powers to the communities."

The agreement also provides that federal and territorial laws are to apply to the settlement area unless they are contrary to the agreement, and that as powers are devolved to the territorial government the Inuvialuit will come under territorial jurisdiction. And the Inuvialuit are declared not to be Indians under section 91(24) of the BNA Act.

Of course, the agreement has had its problems. As Roger Gruben put it: "Agreement signing is easy, the implementation issue is the big one. Governments tend to wash their hands off you once the agreement is signed, they may even suggest cutting programs, saying, 'We've settled with you, so now you can pay for things.' Then there's the issue of setting up the necessary structures and the issue of how you deal with beneficiaries."

A 1989 report of the Sustainable Development Research Group of the Arctic Institute of North America has looked at the difficulty of setting up these structures. It observed:

Limited investment opportunities in the region and high beneficiary expectation are causing some dissatisfaction.

With access to a small pool of trained beneficiaries to fill staff positions, IDC has had to rely on outside consultants for advice. This reliance is necessary during the implementation period of a settled claim but may become problematic if a parallel program is not provided to eventually replace consulting talent with local expertise.

The Quebec Inuit

The James Bay and Northern Quebec Agreement has not been as generous to the Inuit or the Cree of northern Quebec. It has been marked by unhappiness and frustration on the part of the Cree and Inuit, and continues to be a source of frustration as the Quebec government develops plans to proceed with the James Bay II (Great Whale) project.

The Inuit of Quebec for the most part live north of the 55th parallel, land carved out of the North-West Territory in 1912 and transferred to Quebec. While the Quebec Inuit were the subject of more than one federal-provincial dispute, in large measure they were ignored until the James Bay hydroelectric project became reality. Until World War II, the most significant presence in northern Quebec was the Hudson's Bay Company, which in part explains the tendency of the area's Inuit and Cree to use English instead of French as their non-Aboriginal language.

As in many parts of the north, World War II brought the American military to northern Quebec. Fort Chimo, which started out as an HBC trading post, became a major staging base for the American Air Force. (Now known as Kuujjuaq, it is the major administrative centre of Inuit Quebec.)

But the grounds for the biggest change were laid in the 1960s, when a young Liberal cabinet minister by the name of René Lévesque was put in charge of Quebec's water resources. That work led to the James Bay power project and an accompanying agreement, forced on the government by threat of court action, with northern Quebec's Cree and Inuit people.

That agreement gave ownership of 8,737 square kilometres (3,130 square miles) to fifteen Inuit community corporations with a population of approximately five thousand. Mineral rights remained with the Quebec government but could only be exploited with the consent of the Inuit community corporation and upon payment of compensation. In addition, the Inuit were given exclusive hunting and fishing rights over some 98,398 square kilometres. Total compensation paid to Aboriginal parties exceeded $225 million, of which the federal government paid $42,250,000. The Inuit received some $90 million, approximately 40 percent of the total. It is payable to the Inuit Development Corporation, known as Makivik, with final payment to be made in 1999. Under the agreement, Inuit communities set up enrolment committees to determine who were Inuit for the purposes of the agreement.

By choice of the Inuit, their communities became public municipal governments under Quebec municipalities legislation. The Cree, on the other hand, chose to make their communities into Indian reserves under the Indian Act. By choosing public government the Inuit accepted a form of government in which they could become minorities in their communities and lose control of the government if there was a significant migration into northern Quebec. The Cree, on the other hand, like all Indians on reserves, can decide who lives on the reserves.

The Inuit villages have powers over zoning, building permits, public health, parks, recreation, culture, public works, regulation of traffic and taxation. The villages are subject to the Kativik Regional Government, which has the same powers over areas that are beyond village boundaries. It also has powers over the region's policing, transport and communications, and can establish minimum standards (to which all villages are subject) for building and road construction, pollution, sewage and sanitation. Since 1981 the Quebec government has assumed responsibility for delivery of housing and municipal services to the Inuit, with the federal government helping to defray some of the cost.

Many people have not been happy with this arrangement. They complain that the Quebec government supervises the activities of their governments too closely and that all budgets are approved on a line-by-line basis (most of the funding comes from the provincial government) rather than globally. In short, they do not view the arrangement as true self-government, and so have begun negotiating a new governmental arrangement.

The Makivik Corporation is another significant creation of the James Bay Agreement. It was created to receive compensation under the agreement and invest it in a way that will improve the living conditions of the Inuit. In fact, under the terms of the agreement the corporation has to invest a significant portion of the compensation in insurance and trust companies. However, it has also entered into a number of businesses. It undertook a shrimp harvesting venture and a construction company, and it owns Air Inuit and First Air, a major airline in the north.

Under the agreement, responsibility for education in Inuit territory rests with the Kativik School Board, established by provincial legislation. The federal government provides 25 percent of the funding for the board, whose members are elected locally. The agreement stipulates that Inuktitut is one of the languages of instruction in the schools.

The Makivik Corporation has experienced difficulties as well as successes. The corporate structure was alien to a great many people. There is some resentment that the corporation competes with the Inuit co-operative movement; communities where the co-operative movement is strong have been prominent among those Inuit communities that refused to sign the James Bay Agreement. Speaking at a conference to mark the tenth anniversary of the signing of the James Bay Agreement, Harry Tulugak, executive secretary to the Federation of Cooperatives of New Quebec, said:

> What economic development has taken place in Northern Quebec during the last ten years is confined almost exclusively to the growth of the Northern bureaucracies. The private sector pales into insignificance. In 1973, 43 cents of every dollar earned in Northern Quebec was generated through work carried on within the framework of the cooperative movement; by 1981 this had dwindled to a mere 19 cents.
>
> Cooperatives and private businesses which have to struggle for every penny they earn through hard and tedious work just can't function effectively in an atmosphere unfavourable to the business ethic, where the tone is set by organizations whose chief concern is how to "get

more funding" and how to spend money, not how to earn it.

The hardest blow came to the corporation when in 1987 residents rejected the corporation, and other bodies created under the James Bay Agreement, as their agent in preparing a new constitution for regional self-government for the Inuit. In 1983 they had been promised a form of self-government by Premier René Lévesque if they spoke with one voice.

Instead, a six-person committee was elected in 1989 to work on a constitution for a future regional government for northern Quebec. After consulting all fourteen Inuit communities, the committee proposed a regional charter which would guarantee Inuktitut as an official language, recognize the Inuit as a distinct society and guarantee priority for Inuit hunting rights. There would be a regional assembly of twenty members and a separate court system to handle civil matters and some criminal matters. A referendum was held in April 1991, in which the residents of northern Quebec approved, in a 570 to 96 vote (with a 22 percent turnout) the concept of a regional assembly and a constitution. This will be the first such regional government in Canada when it is elected in 1993. This government will not be an Inuit government, but a public one. As long as the Inuit form the majority of the population in the area, they will control the government.

In spite of its benefits, the James Bay Agreement has sparked plenty of dissatisfaction in both the Inuit and Cree camps. Disputes between Ottawa and Quebec, and perhaps a reluctance on Quebec's part to treat the agreement seriously, made the lack of an implementation strategy painfully evident. Coupled with that was the appearance that governments were renouncing any further responsibility for social programs in northern Quebec under the pretext that all that was covered by the agreement.

Criticisms of the agreement came often and from many sources. The Sustainable Development Research Group report, *Coping with Cash*, identified some basic problems with the James Bay Agreement:

There was no advance implementation policy. Northern Quebec is a region with limited investment opportunity and no significant natural resources. An extensive bureaucracy has been created; there is a lack of skilled Native people to administer the claim. The governing structures left little room for individual action; this has inhibited small business development.

Speaking to the House of Commons Standing Committee on Indian and Northern Affairs in 1981, Charlie Watt, one of the Inuit negotiators of the agreement, said:

As the Inuit in the north of Quebec, we thought that we were going to get a benefit out of the Agreement when we signed it. We thought the promise of no cuts in programs would be respected, but the government has not put any substantial amount of financing in over the last seven years. If you compared our communities with the Northwest Territories—the level of services and the necessary needs that should be in the communities—the people would wonder whether we are in a different country.

A 1982 federal review of the implementation of the agreement commented on the condition of Inuit schools:

Many of the school facilities are seriously inadequate. Many of the buildings are seriously overcrowded, lack proper sanitation and fire protection facilities and are in general disrepair. Many of the buildings used as schools were not intended as such and have not been properly adapted for school use. Some do not even provide adequate basic shelter let alone a proper learning environment.

At the conference marking the tenth anniversary of the agreement, Mary Simon, a former Makivik Corporation president, remarked on the delay in having the agreement's provisions carried out. This she attributed to "a lack of cooperation between Canada and Quebec, and ... the unwillingness of governments to meet their financial obligations."

The 1982 federal review, while concluding that "Canada has not breached the Agreement as a matter of law," admitted that "many of the key obligations assumed by Canada are worded in such a way as to give Canada wide discretion in fulfilling them." As a result of this report the federal government spent over $29 million in Inuit communities improving health, housing and sanitation.

Because the agreement was negotiated under considerable pressure—Quebec insisted that the James Bay hydroelectric project had to go ahead on an urgent basis—many of the provisions are vague and subject to widely varying interpretations. It was assumed that everything would be worked out on a co-operative basis once the agreement was in place.

That didn't happen for several reasons. First, there was a sense in some government circles that too much had already been spent on the Inuit and Cree of James Bay. Quebec especially was a reluctant participant in the negotiations—taking part only because of the threat of court action. Coupled with this was the jurisdictional rivalry between Ottawa and Quebec.

At this point, the agreement's greatest weakness became apparent: there was no mechanism to ensure that all the provisions are carried out by governments and it imposes no sanctions if the governments fail to act.

Some legal scholars have argued that both the federal and provincial governments owe a fiduciary duty to Native people to protect their best interest. The concept of a fiduciary obligation stems from the 1984 Supreme Court decision which found against the federal government in favour of the Musqueam Indian Band in Vancouver. They say that, based on such a theory, the Aboriginal people of the James Bay area could sue the two governments for failing to live up to their commitments.

Belatedly, governments acted to try to correct some of the most obvious problems. The federal government has entered into negotiations for an implementation agreement with the Inuit. And in 1987 Quebec and the federal government signed a memorandum of understanding to harmonize their economic development programs in the James Bay area. Quebec has also entered into negotiations with the Makivik Corporation to look at implementation of the agreement.

But matters have become complicated with Quebec's plan to proceed with the Great Whale project. While the Cree have been solidly against the project, the Inuit have split on how to deal with the government over it. While a great many Inuit oppose the project, in a March 1991 election Senator Charlie Watt was elected president of the Makivik Corporation on a platform which promised to negotiate with Quebec over the project. His position has been that negotiations should continue, to see what the government has to offer before making a final decision on whether to oppose the project. Because of considerable opposition—including international lobbying—there is now some doubt as to whether the project will proceed.

The lessons of James Bay were not lost on the Inuit of the eastern Arctic as they proceeded to settle their claim.

The Eastern Arctic Agreement

"The TFN negotiations were slow, but everything was being thought through as compared to James Bay," Paul Okalik, a member of the Tungavik Federation of Nunavut negotiating team, has said. Another member of the negotiating team pointed out, "Our agreement is a massive document, but it covers all the details." The agreement-in-principle, signed in April 1990, took more than ten years to negotiate and is a mass of details spread over 371 double-spaced pages. The final agreement that was concluded in January 1992 made very few changes to this document. The agreement-in-principle, in fact, represented a series of sub-agreements negotiated since the early 1980s; the first, dealing with wildlife, was signed in October 1981. Initial implementation of some of the sub-agreements even started before the agreement-in-principle was signed. The protracted negotiations proceeded at a friendly pace, unlike negotiations of other land claims. "We had joint Christmas parties and barbecues with the federal team," one of the TFN's negotiating team recalled.

Under the agreement, the Inuit will retain approximately 352,000 square kilometres of land, 36,257 square kilometres of which includes mineral rights. This amounts to approximately 9.9 percent of the 2.6 million square kilometres traditionally used by the seventeen thousand Inuit of the eastern Arctic. While not as generous as the Inuvialuit agreement, this agreement is probably the second most generous land claim settlement to be signed, setting aside approximately 15.5 square kilometres per person. It covers all of the eastern Arctic west of the Inuvialuit final settlement area and includes all of the Arctic islands except for the western half of Victoria Island, Banks Island, Prince Patrick Island, the western half of Melville Island and most of Borden and Mackenzie King Island. Those islands fall within the Inuvialuit Final Agreement.

The land set aside for the Inuit, including the mineral rights, is to be parcelled out between the six regions (North Baffin, South Baffin, Keewatin, Kitikmeot East, Kitikmeot West and Sanikiluaq) identified in the agreement. Land is to be held by Inuit organizations designated by the TFN in the form in which private owners in the rest of Canada own land. Such organizations cannot sell their interest in land except to the government, for the primary purpose of such lands is to ensure "economic self-sufficiency of Inuit through time." Communities were given a say in selecting the land they wanted. Each community had a Community Land Identification Negotiating Team (CLINT) composed of an elder, a representative of the Hunters and Trappers Organization, the municipal council, the local Inuit association and the TFN regional negotiator to help with the land selection. At least 75 percent of the land selected was land identified by the community organization. High Arctic lands were exempt from selection, as were lands held privately. In making their selection the Inuit were given the right to select lands that contain carving stone. Land selection had been completed by 1992, with the transfer pending ratification of the final agreement.

Every Inuk is given the right to remove up to 50 cubic yards of carving stone per year from Crown lands. The Inuit are also given the exclusive right to use any water flowing through their lands. No development project in either the NWT or the Nunavut area can be approved if it will affect the quality or quantity of water flowing through the Inuit lands unless a compensation agreement has first been achieved. Inuit lands are not subject to taxation, unless they have improvements on them, in which case they are subject to the same taxation as other lands with improvements. Commercial users who want access to Inuit lands or need access to subsurface minerals must first negotiate with the Inuit, and failing that obtain an order from the Surface Rights Tribunal. Before land is opened to petroleum exploration by the government the local Inuit are to be consulted.

The agreement grants the Inuit $580 million compensation in 1989 dollars payable over a fourteen-year period. The Inuit also get 50 percent of the first $2 million and 5 percent thereafter (by comparison, the Dene/Métis were offered 10 percent under their agreement) of all royalties earned from Nunavut lands. There is a cap on royalty payments; in no case may they result in an average Inuit per capita income exceeding the Canadian average income.

All monies received both from the settlement and resource development are to be paid to the Nunavut Trust, an Inuit-run organization composed of trustees selected by each regional Inuit organization. The Trust is required to invest the monies and may pay dividends to beneficiaries. Income earned by the Trust is subject to taxation, as are benefits paid out by the Trust to individual beneficiaries.

Beneficiaries under the agreement are determined by the Inuit themselves. Each community has an enrolment committee to determine who is an Inuk. Education, health and welfare issues are not dealt with in the agreement. The territorial government took the position that these issues were within its jurisdiction. However, the agreement provides for a Nunavut Social Development Council to provide Inuit with a vehicle for input into social and cultural policies. The agreement also calls for the creation of an Inuit Heritage Trust to assume responsibility for supporting, maintaining and restoring, and displaying archaeological sites, specimens and archives. The agreement also stipulates that the government will put into place a permit requirement for anyone wanting to protect, excavate and restore archaeological sites (this is already required by the NWT government). The Trust is also charged with the responsibility of reviewing place names in the Nunavut area and changing them to traditional Inuit place names.

There are extensive social and economic benefits for Inuit under the agreement. The agreement provides for proportional representation for Inuit in the public service. Each government agency is to develop a plan to increase Inuit employment to the point that they will eventually have proportionate representation in the public service. Job descriptions for public service positions are to be changed to require an "understanding of the social and cultural milieu of the Nunavut Settlement Area," which includes a knowledge of Inuit culture and fluency in Inuktitut. Training programs for government positions are to be community-based where possible, or are to rotate within the communities and be conducted in Inuktitut.

Unless waived by the Inuit, every major development must be preceded by an Inuit Impact and Benefit Agreement (IIBA). This covers power generation anywhere in the eastern Arctic and non-renewable resource extraction wholly or partly from Inuit lands. An IIBA is required only if the project will employ more than two hundred person-years or involve the expenditure of $35 million (in 1986 dollars) over a five-year period.

The Inuit are also given significant involvement in land-use planning, environmental impact assessments and wildlife management. The agreement creates a Nunavut Wildlife Management Board with nine members, four of whom are Inuit appointees, and chaired by a government appointee recommended by the board. The board is to act as the main regulator of access to wildlife in the Nunavut area and is empowered to conduct wildlife studies, establish harvest levels and ascertain the basic needs level and allocation of game. The board is also required to promote and encourage training for Inuit in wildlife research and management. In allocating wildlife quotas a set of priorities is set out, with first priority going to meet basic Inuit food needs, second to meet personal consumption needs by other permanent residents, next for existing sport and commercial operations, then for economic ventures by the local Inuit Hunters and Trappers organizations and Regional Wildlife Organizations, and finally for other commercial use. If there is insufficient game to meet those priorities, only Inuit needs are to be met. Each Inuit community can set up a Hunters and Trappers Organization to allocate the quota assigned to the community and to regulate harvesting practices and techniques among members. Those organizations can in turn join to form Regional Wildlife Organizations. The agreement also stipulates that all leases of Crown land to developers will include a clause that the lease is subject to the prior right of the Inuit to enter into the land to exercise their hunting rights. Each Inuk is assured the right to harvest up to his or her limit of basic needs without the requirement of any permit, and the right to sell or barter any game.

Inuit hunting rights in Nunavut are subject to international agreements (such as agreements on migratory birds and whaling). But under the Eastern Arctic Agreement the federal government has undertaken to try to change any international agreements that limit Inuit rights and to avoid entering into future agreements which might limit Inuit rights. The federal government has also agreed to involve Inuit in studies and negotiations pertaining to such agreements.

A developer whose activities result in an Inuk hunter losing equipment, income or game for personal use is liable for that loss, regardless of whether the developer was at fault. The claimant can either go to court or to a Surface Rights Tribunal to ensure payment.

The Inuit are also given the right to establish outpost camps whose internal operation and management is left to the Inuit applying Inuit customary law.

The agreement also provides for Inuit involvement in the planning and management of any federal or territorial parks in the Nunavut area.

In addition to the Nunavut Wildlife Board and the Surface Rights Tribunal, the agreement provides for a number of other boards. All boards are required to have permanent offices in Nunavut, to meet in Nunavut and to hear representations in Inuktitut.

The Nunavut Planning Policy Committee is responsible for broad policy planning regarding the conservation, development and management of land in Nunavut. The federal and territorial governments have equal representation with Inuit on the committee.

The Nunavut Planning Commission's role is to ensure that development plans conform with land use plans established by the committee and to monitor such developments.

An equally important body is the Nunavut Impact Review Board (NIRB). The board's primary function is to rule on whether projects need to be reviewed to determine their impact on the region and its people, and to advise on what terms and conditions project proposals should proceed. The board is a joint Inuit/government board, with four Inuit representatives, two federal representatives and two territorial representatives. It is required to mandate a review when a development is likely to have significant effects on the environment and on harvesting activities, to have adverse socio-economic effects on northerners or cause significant public concern, or when it involves unknown technological innovations. If required, the review is to be carried out either by the Federal Environmental Assessment panel or by the NIRB itself. The federal government can reject the board's report on the basis of overriding national or regional interest or on the basis that the terms and conditions are more onerous than necessary or are insufficient to mitigate environmental and social impacts.

The NIRB also has a monitoring function to ensure that all terms and conditions are complied with. However, actual enforcement of the terms and conditions is left to the interested government departments.

Also established under the agreement is a joint Inuit/government Nunavut Water Board, whose responsibilities are to regulate and manage the use of inland water in the Nunavut territory. If a project involves both land and water use then the board is to co-operate with other agencies working on the project review.

Because the Inuit have used offshore waters, especially ice zones permanently contiguous to the land, many of the provisions of the agreement apply offshore. These include those parts of the agreement dealing with wildlife, wildlife compensation, conservation, land use planning and resource sharing. As well, Canada recognizes in the agreement that its sovereignty over the waters of the Arctic archipelago is supported by Inuit use and occupancy.

There are a number of other broad principles set out in the agreement. The agreement makes clear that the Inuit are to continue to be able to benefit from any general programs established for the benefit of all Aboriginal people, and from any future rights established on behalf of Aboriginal people under the constitution. The agreement does not prevent the devolution of power to the territorial government or the creation of a future province, provided that these do not lessen Inuit rights under the agreement.

At the time of writing, the final agreement remained to be ratified; a vote was set for early November 1992. All Inuit aged sixteen and older may vote. While the agreement has received considerable support, it has also faced opposition, especially from Inuit who have questioned its requirement that they surrender Aboriginal title. The agreement calls on the Inuit to "cede, release and surrender ... all their aboriginal claims, rights, title and interest" and "not to assert any cause of action, action for a declaration, claim or demand against ... Canada or any province, the government of any territory or any person based on any aboriginal claims, rights, title ..." Nunatsiaq MP Jack Anawak, in a letter to the editor published in the *Nunatsiaq News*, wrote, "I question whether Inuit have to extinguish their rights in order to get Nunavut."

At this time, the full extent of Aboriginal rights remains undefined. Based on court decisions to date, these rights include the right to use the land in hunting and fishing for food and commercial purposes and for religious purposes. But the full implications of Aboriginal title remain unknown. Does it, for example, include absolute ownership to surface and subsurface rights? If so, say opponents of the Eastern Arctic Agreement, the Inuit should not surrender their rights so easily. It was this reasoning that prompted the Dene/Métis of the NWT to reject their 1990 agreement with the federal government. "Our rights are entrenched with the Canadian Constitution; Supreme Court cases are beginning to define those rights and we as Dene are not prepared to give up any of those treaty or aboriginal rights," Bill Erasmus, Dene president, said in a 1990 interview with *The Globe and Mail*.

This position has prompted many Aboriginal people to rethink negotiating strategies. One Inuk woman from Rankin Inlet put it this way: "A lot of people will only vote to give up Aboriginal title if we are guaranteed Nunavut." A simple settlement of land claims will no longer suffice for them.

What the Eastern Arctic Agreement Means to the Inuit

Perhaps the most important aspect of the agreement is that it turns Nunavut over to the Inuit. Aside from the provisions of Article 4—in which all parties to the agreement reiterate their support for the creation of Nunavut—the agreement makes Nunavut into an Inuit territory in many practical ways. It makes Inuktitut a language of business in Nunavut; it creates a series of structures to manage resources and plan development in which the Inuit will have significant input; it will make the public service in Nunavut an Inuit one; and it will ensure an Inuit voice in the development and preservation of cultural sites.

While the agreement will inject considerable cash into the economy, it may not make Nunavut into an economically self-sufficient territory. The *Scone Report* made clear that the belief that land claims will solve the north's economic woes is "a myth of the first order." As the report pointed out, the uncertainty of investing in the north means that many Native groups are being advised to invest elsewhere, where a surer return can be expected.

That conclusion was supported by the Sustainable Development Research Group: "Experiences in Alaska, James Bay and Northern Quebec, and in the Inuvialuit region of the Northwest Territories indicate there are few, if any, immediate and direct benefits occurring to beneficiaries of claims settlements."

There are other major issues which will have to be resolved as the agreement is implemented. Within Nunavut there will be lands controlled specifically by Inuit people and their boards. Will this mean that some lands will be subject to three levels of jurisdiction—that of the Inuit, that of the territorial government (or Nunavut, should it come to be) and that of the federal government? The agreement provides that in event of a conflict of law, the agreement will prevail over federal and territorial legislation. If Nunavut becomes reality, will there in fact be two levels of Inuit administration—one under the agreement and another resulting from the public government of Nunavut? While some provisions of the agreement apply to all lands within Nunavut, others apply only to Inuit lands.

What will such a régime mean for resource development? A number of oil companies have complained that the Inuvialuit Final Agreement has resulted in three different régimes in the area— Inuvialuit, territorial and federal—which has made resource development much more difficult. Add to that the complications arising from a project crossing land claims boundaries. As Gary Wagner of the Inuvialuit Environmental Impact Review Board put it: "Assume you have a major pipeline project which crosses several land claims areas—does this mean that one claim area could block something which the people in another area want?"

There are no easy and simple solutions to these difficult questions. Rather, they are the challenging problems that will have to be resolved as political development in the north continues.

If ratified, the agreement will be a major step towards the creation of Nunavut. Even if this agreement is not finalized, the process of land claims negotiations will continue and eventually a final agreement will be reached. Many of the current provisions will undoubtedly find their way into the new agreement: they are things that the Inuit have fought for for decades. And it is a sure bet that any new agreement will have to deal with the issue of Nunavut. Then, as Nunavut develops, a major question that will have to be asked is, What will Nunavut mean for the Inuit in Labrador, in Nunavik (northern Quebec) and in the Mackenzie Delta–Beaufort Sea area? Will the Inuit in those areas look to Nunavut to protect their interests and to speak on their behalf? Will the Inuit of Quebec look to Nunavut to help them resolve disputes under future development projects in northern Quebec?

8

Nunavut and Canada's Future

A Future Scenario: A.D. 2020

"STOP RACISM" the placards carried by the protesters in front of Nunatta Campus in Iqaluit read. "WE SUPPORT FRENCH, SO PLEASE SUPPORT INUKTITUT" other placards read. Yet another reads "NEWFOUNDLAND WE LOVE YOU—SO SUPPORT US."

This interprovincial dispute in the year 2020 centres on education. Many Inuit students from northern Quebec and Labrador have been attending Nunatta campus rather than universities in their own provinces. For the students from northern Quebec, Iqaluit is geographically much closer than the universities of southern Quebec. Equally important for many Inuit students from Labrador and Quebec is the fact that the physical and cultural climate in Iqaluit is much more comparable to their homes than that found in urban centres such as Montreal, Quebec, Sherbrooke or St. John's, Newfoundland. Of even greater importance to many students is that one-third of the instruction in Nunatta is in Inuktitut and that there are classes in Inuit history and culture. The cultural and linguistic program at Nunatta is bolstered by a faculty/student exchange that that institution has with a similar institution in Nuuk, Greenland.

Of course, no student in Canada is denied the right to study at a university in a province other than her home province. Nor in this current dispute is anyone denying Quebec and Labrador students the right to study in Iqaluit. What is at stake is money.

For years, starting in the mid-1960s, the federal government has provided grants to the provinces under its established program financing (EPF) to support higher education. The Nunavut Department of Education has asked Ottawa to turn over a share of the EPF paid to Quebec and Newfoundland for education to itself. The department has argued that because most Inuit post-secondary students from those provinces attend Nunatta campus, a portion of funding should go to Nunavut because it is serving the Inuit residents of those provinces.

Matters have been further complicated by a test case launched in the Federal Court of Canada. A student from Nain, Labrador applied to Nunatta and was turned down because the campus did not have sufficient financial resources. She is now suing the federal government, arguing that some of the federal transfer payment should go to Nunavut to support her studies at Nunatta, and her cause is supported by the Nunavut government. Her lawyers argue that the federal refusal to pay some of the EPF funds designated for Newfoundland to Nunavut is interfering with her mobility rights under section 6(2) of the Charter of Rights and Freedoms, and further argue that the federal decision will prevent her "from gaining of a livelihood" in a province because she wants to teach Inuit children in Inuktitut and the only place she can gain the training is in Iqaluit.

Both the governments of Newfoundland and Quebec have applied to intervene in the dispute. Both the Quebec and the Newfoundland premiers have warned Ottawa against interfering with the transfer payment scheme because they alone have the jurisdiction over education. The dispute has been going on for some five years. Initially, Nunavut approached the Quebec and Newfoundland governments for an agreement wherein Nunavut would provide higher education to their Inuit residents in return for appropriate financial compensation.

The possibility of Nunavut raises many complex and challenging questions, including those posed by the above scenario. Can the governments of Newfoundland and Quebec truly speak for their Inuit citizens, who are a small minority in each case, or would the task best be handled by the Inuit government of Nunavut? Of course, to turn the task over might involve restructuring provincial boundaries or at least redefining how provinces operate. It also raises the question of whether a province should be a voice for one ethnic constituency. If Nunavut becomes the voice of the Inuit, are other Aboriginal groups likely to seek such an arrangement? If so, what does this mean for the current federal-provincial power arrangement in Canada? One could argue that, in fact, the question of a province assuming the role of protector of an ethnic group has already been resolved, with Quebec having assumed that role for the French language and culture in North America. And some Inuit argue that had the boundaries of Quebec not been extended northward by the federal government in 1912, Nunavik—the Inuit lands of northern Quebec—would in fact be part of the NWT and would fall within the proposed Nunavut.

Should an Inuit government—or for that matter any Aboriginal government—have a responsibility for members of its cultural community outside its territorial jurisdiction? As self-government proceeds down the road to reality—albeit at an extremely slow pace—the issue of jurisdiction of such a government for its people beyond its boundaries is an issue which has yet to be resolved. Is the creation of a province such as Nunavut likely to lead to calls for provincehood by other groups, especially other Aboriginal communities? If so, will this mean the redrawing of provincial boundaries?

There are a great many other questions to pose here. Are there parallels between the situation of the Inuit of the eastern Arctic and the Métis of Manitoba? The Métis also fought for provincehood in 1870, which they obtained but subsequently lost. What does Nunavut mean for the rest of the north? Will Nunavut affect our foreign affairs as the Inuit seek to strengthen contacts with Inuit in other countries?

These unanswered questions should not be seen as obstacles to political development in the north. Rather, they are questions that Canadians need to consider as northern development unfolds. And in view of the redefinition of Canada that is now taking place, this is an opportune time to examine some of these questions.

Probably one of the most difficult questions to resolve is the relationship of Nunavut to the Inuit outside of the eastern Arctic.

Quebec, Newfoundland and Nunavut

In the aftermath of the failed Meech Lake Accord, the Quebec government announced a constitutional commission to look into Quebec's future. The only options rejected by Premier Bourassa were maintaining the status quo and joining the United States. When that commission, the Bélanger-Campeau Commission, reported, it called for a referendum on sovereignty unless there was a federal proposal forthcoming that would see massive transfer of power to the Quebec government. While leaving considerable discretion to the government, the Quebec National Assembly passed legislation allowing for a referendum on sovereignty or on any federal offer. Tentatively, that referendum was scheduled to be held by the fall of 1992. Following the report of that commission, the Quebec government appointed a number of other bodies to study, among other things, the costs of separation and the possibilities of renewed federalism.

The questions arises: if Quebec significantly redefines its relationship with Canada, can it also do so for its Aboriginal citizens, particularly those who occupy the northern part of the province?

The Inuit territory has only been a part of Quebec for approximately eighty years, having been transferred to Quebec in 1912. The transfer of this land from the North-West Territory to Quebec was made on condition that "the trusteeship of the Indians in the said territory ... shall remain in the Government of Canada." By legislation passed that year, Quebec accepted this condition.

A 1939 Supreme Court of Canada decision ruled that Inuit were Indians under section 91(24) of the BNA Act and therefore a federal responsibility. That section puts "Indians, and lands reserved for Indians" in federal jurisdiction. (Before 1939 it had been unclear whether Inuit fell into that category.) The Supreme Court decision was the culmination of a dispute as to who should pay for relief for the Inuit of northern Quebec.

Ironically, each side in that dispute was seeking to shed its responsibility upon the other. In a 1929 agreement, Ottawa and Quebec had agreed that Ottawa would provide relief for the Inuit but would be reimbursed by Quebec. For three years, Quebec paid Ottawa nine dollars per person per year. But in 1932 the Quebec government, led by Premier Taschereau, questioned whether it was obliged to pay for Inuit relief. Quebec argued that the Inuit were Indians under section 91(24) of the constitution and therefore a federal responsibility.

In deciding that Eskimos (as the Inuit were then referred to) were Indians under section 91(24) of the BNA Act, the Supreme Court looked at what the term "Indian" meant in 1867. The Court attached considerable significance to a Hudson's Bay Company census of the mid-1850s which counted 4,000 "Esquimaux" as part of the 147,000 Indians living under its jurisdiction. The Court also looked at various official documents. For example, in General Murray's 1762 report on "Indian nations residing within the government [of Quebec]," Murray states: "In order to discuss this point more clearly I shall first take notice of the Savages on the North shore ... The first to be met with on this side are the Esquimaux." The Court also noted correspondence from the 1870s, which documented that Ottawa had taken on the role of providing relief for the Inuit of northern Quebec. In 1879 the Vicar General of Rimouski had petitioned federal minister Hector Langevin for further federal relief for the "esquimaux" of northern Quebec. Langevin directed the complaint to Prime Minister John A. Macdonald, who turned the request over to his Deputy Superintendent of Indian Affairs. He, in turn, replied that the department had in fact sought a larger budget in order to be able to grant larger relief to these people. It was on the basis of these points that the Court concluded that the term "Indian" included the Eskimo.

This decision did not end the dispute forever. Initially, Quebec was happy to let the federal government provide health and education services to the Inuit. The RCMP even patrolled the area. However, with the election of the Lesage government in 1960 and the advent of the Quiet Revolution, things began to change. Northern Quebec was seen as having great potential for mineral and hydroelectric development. Such developments, the thinking went, could transform Quebec into a prosperous industrial society. So, in the 1960s, Quebec began to question Ottawa's jurisdiction over the Inuit. It argued that it should be able to provide the same services to the Inuit that were provided to other Quebeckers and receive compensation from Ottawa. An agreement to that effect was reached in 1969.

Quebec continued to act on its need to assert jurisdiction over the north. Speaking at a conference marking the tenth anniversary of the signing of the James Bay Agreement, Quebec Inuit leader Mark Gordon said:

The institutions we created to try to develop autonomy in our area have ended up with what is probably a bigger army of bureaucrats in the South than we have in the North to deliver the services ... What we are ending up with is parallel structures in everything that we try to do in the North. A perfect example of this is the build-up of an empty ghost-town called Radisson. Why did they put people up there? It's so that we could have some people from Quebec City holding the flag in the North.

The James Bay Agreement allowed Quebec to increase its toehold over its northern frontier substantially. Inuit villages, education and health fall under Quebec jurisdiction. So too, plans for self-government have been developed with the Quebec government, with such governments to be clearly within the jurisdiction of Quebec.

However, the argument has been made that, both under the Constitution Act of 1867 and as a result of the special trust obligation that exists, the relationship of Aboriginal people is with the federal government. As already pointed out, Inuit are a federal responsibility under the constitution. A 1984 Supreme Court decision further ruled that there is a federal trust obligation to look after the Aboriginal interest in land. Therefore, the argument goes, the Quebec government cannot speak for the Aboriginal people of northern Quebec. Further, taking into account the international right of self-determination, the question arises of whether Quebec can truly purport to speak for another people. This was a point that Ovide Mercredi, Grand Chief of the Assembly of First Nations, argued when he appeared before a committee of the National Assembly of Quebec.

Assuming, therefore, that there is a substantial redefinition of Canada and that Nunavut becomes reality, is Nunavut likely to have some pull on the allegiance of the Inuit of northern Quebec? Is it not reasonable that the Inuit of northern Quebec should look to Nunavut as a vehicle for the protection and future growth of Inuit culture and language? It should be remembered that there have been contacts between the Inuit of northern Quebec and Baffin Island, including some intermarriage.

It is clear that the possibility for conflict exists, and in any redefinition of Canada this type of situation has to be considered.

The situation of Aboriginal people in Newfoundland has been equally uncertain. When Newfoundland entered Confederation in 1949 the terms of union were silent on any obligation for Aboriginal people and their land. This was in contrast to the terms under which B.C. had entered Confederation: that province undertook to make land available so that reserves could be set aside. So too, when the boundaries of Quebec and Ontario were extended, and when natural resources were transferred to the Prairie governments, there was an undertaking to make land available to settle outstanding Aboriginal claims—and in the case of Quebec and Ontario to actually settle the claims. Why the difference in terms for Newfoundland? Richard Bartlett, in *Indian Reserves and Aboriginal Lands in Canada*, remarked that the negotiators intended that the matter of lands for Aboriginal people be negotiated once a provincial government had been elected in Newfoundland. He further concluded that the federal government itself was uncertain as to the position of Indians and Inuit in Newfoundland. Several opinions suggested that the federal government had a responsibility for Indians and Inuit, but a 1962 opinion from the Minister of Citizenship and Immigration found that Newfoundland's Aboriginal peoples were in fact enfranchised (a legal process whereby status is lost under the Indian Act) and were like all other citizens of Newfoundland.

Nevertheless, the federal government undertook some responsibility for the Newfoundland Aboriginal community and, starting in 1954, entered into a series of five-year agreements wherein it assumed financial responsibility for the Indians and Inuit of Newfoundland and Labrador. While the federal government paid for programs, they were administered by the province.

After threats of lawsuits and pressure from the federal government, Newfoundland reluctantly agreed to enter into land claims negotiations, including that of the Labrador Inuit Association. Newfoundland's December 1987 land claims policy made clear that the federal government was responsible for any financial compensation, but that Newfoundland would provide the land.

While the Newfoundland government has agreed to negotiate land claims, there is no reason to believe that it would be willing to forgo its jurisdiction over the Inuit of Labrador if Nunavut came to be. In fact, the land claims policy makes clear that the province remains "the guarantor of the rights and interests of all provincial residents."

In some small way, Manitoba may also have an interest in the Inuit quest for Nunavut. While the Inuit population of Manitoba are largely recent migrants living in Churchill, the area from Churchill to the NWT border has been traditional Inuit territory.

Not surprisingly, some provinces may face the creation of Nunavut with some reluctance, particularly if it might lead to a fully fledged province. While the rules regarding accession to provincehood are the same whether the NWT is divided or not, if division does occur it may well be that Quebec and Newfoundland will have more concerns than other provinces at the prospect of an Inuit province.

Parallels Between the Manitoba Métis and the Inuit of Nunavut

If the Inuit achieve provincehood, or at least a special territory, the question has to be asked as to whether they will end up in the same situation as the Manitoba Métis today. In settling Inuit claims it is important that future grievances not be created. Today, it is accepted by historians that in attempting to settle the claim of the Manitoba Métis in 1870 the federal government created more problems than it solved, problems that are even more difficult to settle today.

There are many parallels between the Inuit struggle for Nunavut and the struggle of the Métis in Manitoba. At one constitutional conference dealing with Aboriginal issues, Métis delegates urged Inuit to take heed of the Manitoba lesson. Such a comparison has been made by many commentators since. In analysing the developments leading to the creation of Nunavut, a comparison with the early history of Manitoba is worthwhile to determine if the Inuit might end up in the same situation as the Manitoba Métis.

In 1870 the Métis formed well over 80 percent of Manitoba's population, the same proportion that Inuit form of the eastern

Arctic population today. At that time the Métis sought, as the Inuit do today, to exercise their right of self-government through a form of public government. That means a government in which non-Aboriginals have an equal right to participate.

Besides responsible government in the form of provincehood, the Métis asked for land, a government that would function in both English and French, and public funding for denominational schooling. Among other things, the Inuit seek a guaranteed land base, the right to use Inuktitut and recognition of Inuit custom in the judicial system. Is there a possibility that the Inuit could end up in the same position as the Métis in Manitoba did over a hundred years ago? To answer that question it is necessary to see what happened in Manitoba and why it happened.

The Manitoba Act, passed by Parliament in 1870, was supposed to embody the settlement reached between the Métis delegation sent to Ottawa during the winter of 1870 and the federal government. The Act met many of the Métis' major demands, including the creation of a separate province, protection for the lands the Métis occupied, settlement of their Aboriginal claim and protection for the French language and for Catholic schools.

Of course, the Manitoba that the Métis envisaged and the one that Ottawa created were somewhat different. Control of public lands, including lands that were to be set aside for the Métis, remained with Ottawa until 1930. And while the Métis were promised certain land rights—nearly 570,000 hectares of land and the right to claim ownership of the riverlots they occupied—the Métis allege that the promise was kept more in the breach than in practice. They allege that the federal government deliberately wanted to disperse the Métis and ensure that Manitoba did not remain a Métis province. This was achieved by introducing legislation and bureaucratic procedures that made it extremely difficult for adult Métis to obtain the land, while at the same time allowing Métis children—who also were major beneficiaries—to dispose of their land in a quick and easy fashion. By 1886 all of the 570,000 hectares had been granted. Less than 20 percent of the eligible Métis beneficiaries actually owned the land they were entitled to. The Métis fared no better in obtaining title to their riverlots. Because they could not obtain the land they were promised many Métis moved west and north.

The French language was not respected either, when legislation passed in 1890 declared Manitoba to be an English-only province. That same year, support for denominational schools was dealt an equal blow with legislation declaring all Manitoba schools to be non-sectarian.

In short, in the space of a decade, Manitoba went from being a province created to meet Métis demands to one where the Métis had become an insignificant element. In 1870, a full 83 percent of Manitoba's 12,000 people were mixed-blood origin, either Métis (6,000) or English-speaking Half-breeds (as they were referred to in those days). Fifteen years later, less than 7 percent of the population were of mixed-blood origin. With the exception of an English-speaking Half-breed, John Norquay, who became premier of Manitoba in 1878, the Métis people did not play a significant role in the political history of Manitoba. They became outcasts in the province they helped create.

Today, the Manitoba Métis allege that government policies and legislative changes that made it more difficult for adults to get land and easier for children to dispose of land were unconstitutional. They argue that in 1871 when the British Parliament amended the British North America Act to approve the creation of Manitoba, it stated that Canada's Parliament could not alter the Manitoba Act. Their argument is that government legislation and policies in fact did change the Manitoba Act. The Métis also argue that the federal and Manitoba governments breached their special trust obligation to ensure that the best interests of the Métis were considered when land was being parcelled out. They hold that the government was aware of the rampant speculation in Métis lands and corrupt practices by government bureaucrats but turned a blind eye to such practices. In the 1980s, the Métis turned to the courts to resolve their grievances; at the time of writing, the matter was still before the courts.

The Métis litigation is not the first time that the courts have had to review events revolving around the creation of Manitoba. In 1891 the Supreme Court of Canada restored the right of Catholic schools to public funding and in 1979 the Court struck down Manitoba's English-only law.

The Inuit have taken note of the many parallels between their own situation and that of the Manitoba Métis, and that accounts for the differences they have achieved in their 1990 agreement. Under the Manitoba scheme, land distribution was to be made to individuals and was in the hands of the federal government. In the case of the Inuit, land is being turned over to community organizations. And under their agreement Inuit lands cannot be sold or transferred, except to the government. No attempt by speculators to acquire their lands could succeed. The land claims agreement also provides a role for Inuit in public decision making and a role for the Inuktitut language.

In order to protect an Inuit role in the public government of Nunavut the Inuit argue for a bill of rights and constitution for the province that will always guarantee a role for Inuit and will protect their language and culture.

Further, the Inuit agreement is probably constitutionally protected. Section 35(1) of the constitution recognizes and affirms "the existing aboriginal and treaty rights of the aboriginal peoples of Canada." A 1984 amendment defined "treaty rights" to include "rights that now exist by way of land claims agreements or may be so acquired." Therefore, the Inuit land agreement could not be changed without a constitutional amendment. Thus the federal government could not make the kind of legislative changes it did to the Manitoba Act—and even those may be illegal.

And unlike Manitoba in the 1870s, there is no pressure from encroaching settlement or resource development. Thus, unlike the Manitoba Métis, the Inuit in the eastern Arctic may have time to take control of the government and to develop the talent to ensure that they don't lose control. Further, the Inuit have been working for at least a decade and a half on plans for Nunavut, so are probably in a better position than the Métis of Manitoba who were forced to develop their position in the space of about six months.

However, is there any reason to believe that the promises in the land claims agreement could not be subverted if there is no political will to ensure that its terms are complied with? One only has to look at the James Bay Agreement for an answer to that. The only protection that the Inuit would have is to go to court and argue that their agreement is part of the

Canadian constitution by virtue of section 35 and therefore cannot be abrogated unilaterally. So in spite of the fact the Inuit are in a stronger position than the one in which the Métis found themselves in 1870, federal good-will is still necessary for Nunavut to survive and prosper.

Nunavut and the North

A matter of importance to Canada is the issue of what will happen to the rest of the north if Nunavut is created.

"Why not merge the Territory of the Yukon and the western part of the Northwest Territories to make one territory and, consequently, an eleventh province?" Thomas Suluk, the MP for Nunatsiaq, asked in the House of Commons in October 1987.

His suggestion is one which has not been widely discussed. A more likely scenario is that upon division the western half of the NWT would become a separate territory, and probably a province, some day. A separate western territory was in fact envisaged by the Diefenbaker and Pearson governments.

The form of the western territory will obviously be influenced by any land claims agreements reached in that area. The Dene and Métis entered into an agreement-in-principle with the federal government over their land claim that would have allowed them to negotiate self-government and allowed the devolution of provincial-type powers to the government of the NWT. The final agreement reached in early 1990 was never ratified, however, as we have seen. Several communities found the surrender of Aboriginal rights unsatisfactory.

Assuming that these self-government arrangements come to fruition, what role does this leave for the government of the NWT? One option that a 1988 GNWT discussion paper on constitutional development proposes is "the federal option" wherein Aboriginal lands are ruled by Aboriginal governments, with the remainder staying under federal jurisdiction. This option could be chosen whether division occurred or not.

To deal with some of these issues, the territorial government appointed a commission in 1991 with the mandate of developing a plan for the western Arctic territory. The commission will have a most difficult task, for unlike the eastern Arctic, there is not a homogeneous population in the west. As already discussed, slightly over half the population is non-Aboriginal. The Aboriginal population is made up of the Dene (further divided into various nations), the Métis and the Inuvialuit—if they become a part of the western territory. Even more seriously, perhaps, the commission is considered by some Dene spokespersons as an insult to the work that was done in the mid-1980s towards the creation of Denendeh. They fear that the western territory will become like southern jurisdictions in which the Aboriginal people have been relegated to a minor role.

International Affairs

The creation of Nunavut will also have a bearing on foreign affairs. As Quebec has sought contact with other francophone nations, so too do Canada's Inuit seek to maintain ties with their cultural sisters in Greenland, Alaska and Russia. In *Building Nunavut*, the Inuit argued:

> It is recommended that the Nunavut government be recognized as having legitimate interests in various international matters and that a Nunavut constitution specify that in cooperation with the Government of Canada it may undertake such international activities as may be agreed from time to time with that Government.

Canada's Inuit are already active in the Inuit Circumpolar Conference (ICC), which represents the world's 100,000 Inuit. That organization grew out of a 1977 meeting at Barrow, Alaska, called by its mayor, Eben Hopson, over concern about what resource development was doing to the Arctic environment. It was formally incorporated in 1980 with these purposes:
- To strengthen unity among Inuit of the circumpolar world.
- To promote Inuit rights and interests on the international level.
- To ensure the endurance and growth of Inuit culture and societies.
- To promote long-term management and protection of Arctic wildlife and environment.

Besides offices in Nuuk, Greenland, and in Anchorage, Alaska, the organization also has an office in Ottawa. It has gained non-governmental organization status at the UN and has made presentations to the UN Working Group on Indigenous Populations on behalf of the Inuit. It has lobbied the International Whaling Commission for recognition of subsistence whaling rights for Inuit people. In addition, it was actively involved in lobbying against the Arctic Pilot Project, which involved liquefying northern natural gas and shipping it south in special tankers. Most recently, it has taken up the cause of protecting the Arctic environment.

There are already precedents for provincial involvement in international affairs. A great many provinces have established offices to represent them abroad. Quebec has played a major role in conferences of francophone nations and has recently gained the right to sit as a separate delegation at such summits.

The Inuit population of Greenland is approximately 44,000, and of Alaska, 30,000. Russia's Inuit population is uncertain, but estimates range from 1,500 to 4,000. Until 1989, the Inuit of the USSR—as the country was then known—were not allowed to participate in the ICC. That year they sent their first delegates to the conference at Sisimiut, Greenland.

An Inuit government representing Canada's 30,000 Inuit is likely to be even more assertive in seeking a voice in international forums where Canada deals with issues touching upon its northern people.

Resource Development

Developments surrounding Inuit land claims and the building of Nunavut will have important implications for Canada's resource development policies. Until now, northern resource development has largely proceeded on the basis of what is best for the south. Now resource development schemes and national dreams of trans-Arctic shipping must take into account a new player, the Inuit people. The Inuit interest can no longer be ignored. Land claims agreements and developments leading to the creation of Nunavut ensure that.

Undoubtedly, the creation of Nunavut will strengthen Canada's claim to the Northwest Passage, as Nunavut will act to protect the interests of its people there. However, there is a

price. Canada may have to concede its ability to proceed unilaterally with resource development and shipping projects
which may be in the national interest but may conflict with
local use of the land and waterways.

Resource development has traditionally been an area of provincial control. In the same way that the federal government
relinquished control over land and resources to the Prairie
provinces in the 1930 Natural Resources Transfer Agreements,
so too it may have to concede similar control to the north. Forty
years after the National Resources Transfer Agreements Ottawa ended up in a fight with Saskatchewan and Alberta when
some of the policies of those provinces dealing with oil and
potash ran counter to the national interest (or, depending on
one's interpretation, when Ottawa's policies ignored the west).
As seen in the opening chapter, a similar fight between Ottawa
and Nunavut is entirely possible.

While shipping and interprovincial movement of goods are
within federal jurisdiction, it is clear that the Inuit are going to
want a say in the movement of resources through their territory, especially when this movement has a potentially significant impact on a great many people and their lifestyle.

More important, the Inuit may have a voice in controlling
development directly. Under their land claims agreement, the
joint Inuit-government Nunavut Impact Review Board will
have the power to review development projects and shipping
connected with any resource development project to determine their "ecosystemic and socio-economic impacts." The
board can determine "whether project proposals should
proceed, and if so, under what terms and conditions."

Of course, some of the development in the Beaufort Sea–
Mackenzie Delta area falls outside the Inuit land claims settlement area and may fall outside the future territory or province
of Nunavut. However, lands in those areas do fall within the
Inuvialuit Final Agreement that gives the Inuvialuit population of approximately 2,500 a similar voice in any developments in their area.

The climate has changed. The Inuit have become significant
players on the national field and the national interest can no
longer ignore their interests. Will Canadians understand this,
or will it take a crisis of the kind outlined in the fictional

scenario at the beginning of this book for them to come to grips with this reality?

Conclusion

Canada is on the verge of significant changes. In part, those changes will come because of Quebec's dissatisfaction with the constitutional status quo. Many westerners as well argue that the current federal structure does not meet their aspirations. Aboriginal communities too have made it clear that they must be major participants in any restructuring of Canada. The summer of 1990—when the Aboriginal community played a significant role in the death of Meech Lake Accord, and when it captured the nation's attention with the blockade of the Mercier Bridge into Montreal, the armed standoff at Oka and blockades of the CN/CP mainlines through northern Ontario—made it clear that the past strategies of dealing with Aboriginal communities would no longer work.

But during that turbulent summer there was one bright spot. Work was proceeding towards finalizing the agreement with the Inuit of the eastern Arctic. Nunavut can be an example that Canada can indeed do things right when it comes to its dealings with Aboriginal people.

There are many significant hurdles that must be overcome to bring Nunavut to reality. Canadian premiers will have to be sold on the merits of a new province. While right now the prospects appear dim for such a development, supporters of Nunavut's provincehood are looking ten to fifteen years into the future; by then there may well be a different atmosphere at the federal-provincial negotiating table. And all Canadians will have to accept that significant federal funding will be needed for Nunavut in the near future.

Nunavut offers Canadians a chance to share in the building of a new Canada. The success of Nunavut will offer a model that might be used in resolving relationships with other Aboriginal groups. More important still, it will be an opportunity to put into reality the Canadian claim to being a truly diverse nation by establishing a territory—or province—in which the language of work, culture and government will not be of European origin.

Sources

In preparing this book I relied on a great many sources of information, including original documents, published books, articles and reports, and personal interviews. Where possible I have tried to acknowledge specific sources in the text. A full list of my printed sources and the lectures I attended appears in the Bibliography of Sources. All of those are sources that helped me gain a better understanding of the issues, and undoubtedly influenced my thinking. Some of those sources were particularly valuable in providing me with background and information on particular sections of the book. As well, a number of individuals provided me with information on specific issues.

In preparing the portion of the text dealing with early Inuit history I found the following works particularly useful: *Canadian Arctic Prehistory* by Robert McGhee; and articles by Charles Arnold entitled "A Summary of the Prehistory of the Western Canadian Arctic" and "Vanishing Villages of the Past: Rescue Archaeology in the Mackenzie Delta." The opening quotation in Chapter 2 comes from the latter article. Also useful was *The Inuit*, published by Indian and Northern Affairs. The article referred to in Chapter 2 dealing with Inuit occupancy of northern Manitoba is "Inuit Land Use and Occupancy in Northern Manitoba" by Roderick Riewe, Luke Suluk and Lorraine Brandson.

Federal government policies and programs for Inuit have been discussed in numerous sources. Those which I found particularly helpful included: *Canada's Colonies* by Kenneth Coates; R. Quinn Duffy's *Road to Nunavut*; and Dr. Richard Diubaldo's *The Government of Canada and the Inuit, 1900–1967*. Hugh Brody's book, *The People's Land*, was another source I relied on to help me understand Inuit history after European contact, the growth of settlements and early government policies towards the Inuit.

A number of sources proved helpful in preparing the section on Canada's assertion of northern sovereignty. Those included: *Politics of the Northwest Passage*, in particular Chapter 2, by Graham Rowley; Shelagh Grant's book, *Sovereignty or Security*; and the works by Coates and Duffy mentioned earlier.

Richard Diubaldo's work was particularly valuable in understanding the health and education situation among the Inuit both before and after World War II. The two short quotations in the section in Chapter 2 dealing with health and education come from his book. His work, along with that of R. Quinn Duffy, was particularly important in understanding Canada's effort to deal with the tuberculosis epidemic in the north. Equally important in that regard was P. Nixon's article, "Early Administrative Developments in Fighting Tuberculosis among Canadian Inuit: Bringing State Institutions Back In."

The book *British Law and Arctic Men* by R. G. Moyle was a most useful background source on the murder trials of Sinnisiak and Uluksuk discussed in Chapter 2. The quotation from prosecutor Charles McCaul's opening address comes from this book. Other information on the trials comes from an article appearing in the November 3, 1917, issue of *The Graphic*, London, England. The quotation from defence lawyer James Wallbridge's address to the jury comes from this article. Details on the murder of Robert Janes, as well as information on other cases, comes from a number of sources, including Ken Coates's *Canada's Colonies*, Hugh Brody's *The People's Land* and R. Quinn Duffy's *Road to Nunavut*. Richard Diubaldo also wrote about all these cases and his work is useful in grasping their details.

Martha Flaherty's comments before the House of Commons Aboriginal Affairs Committee, repeated in Chapter 3, were reported in the Minutes of the Proceedings and Evidence of the Standing Committee on Aboriginal Affairs, March 19, 1990. Remarks made by Annie Padlo, the Inuit translator, are found in a report in *Nunatsiaq News*, November 30, 1990 (p. 1). Diamond Jenness's comments on relocation appeared in "Technical Paper #14, Eskimo Administration in Canada," published by the Arctic Institute of North America in May 1964.

Cecil Lingard's book, *Territorial Government in Canada: The Autonomy Question in the Old North-West Territories*, is an excellent source of information regarding the debate over the creation of the provinces of Alberta and Saskatchewan.

The results of the plebiscite on division, along with the work of the NCF and the WCF, have been documented in many sources. A particularly valuable source is the chronology of events found in *Partners for the Future: A Selection of Papers Related to the Constitutional Development in the Western Northwest Territories*. This publication is also a valuable source of information on the boundary issue. Details regarding the Nunavut Wildlife Advisory Board and the controversy surrounding it come from various news reports appearing in *Nunatsiaq News*.

The quotation by Paul Quassa on devolution that appears in Chapter 5 comes from a *Nunatsiaq News* report of June 1, 1990, "TFN Demands Role in Devolution of Power" (p. 1).

Information on the costs of division in Chapter 5 comes from the GNWT report entitled "Financial Impact of Division," prepared by Coopers & Lybrand in 1991.

Mark Gordon's quotation in Chapter 6 comes from *Aboriginal Self-Government and Constitutional Reform: Setbacks, Opportunities and Arctic Experiences*.

A number of sources were most helpful in giving me an understanding of the current operations of the GNWT. The most important were: a 1988 paper prepared by the GNWT, "A Discussion Paper Prepared by the GNWT on Political and Constitutional Development in the NWT"; a similar report entitled "Seize the Day," presented by the GNWT to the Assembly on October 27, 1989; "A Position Paper on Political and Constitutional Development," presented to the Assembly on February 25, 1991; and the chapter on the Northwest Territories in *Provincial and Territorial Legislatures in Canada* and the report *Strength at Two Levels*.

Information on the activities of the ICC comes from the article "Arctic Policy and Self-Determination: A Canadian Inuit Perspective," published in *IWIGIA*, Document 63, July 1989 at p. 21, and also from a conversation with Corinne Gray, co-ordinator at the ICC's Ottawa office. Peter Jull's article, "Inuit Politics and the Arctic Seas," in *Politics of the Northwest Passage*, was also an important source of information.

Erhard Treude's article, "Eighteenth Century Eskimo Land Cessions in Northern Labrador," was particularly helpful in gaining an understanding of the role of Moravian missionaries in Labrador. The quotation in Chapter 7 dealing with the land negotiations between the Moravians and the Inuit comes from this article. As well, the brief overview of the factual details regarding the Inuit and their dealings with Moravians is based on that article. Toby Andersen, Director of Land Claims, Labrador Inuit Association, updated me on the claim being advanced by the Labrador Inuit.

In understanding the Inuvialuit Final Agreement, Janet Keeping's book *The Inuvialuit Final Agreement* was most helpful, as was Richard Bartlett's *Indian Reserves and Aboriginal Lands in Canada: A Homeland*. I learned a number of useful points from Andrew Thompson's January 15, 1990, lecture in Saskatoon entitled "Northern Land Claims Settlements: Contemporary Nation Building." Professor Peter Cumming provided me with considerable background information. Especially useful were meetings with Roger Gruben, Chairman, Inuvialuit Regional Corporation; Anne Matheson, Executive Assistant to that corporation; and Gary Wagner of the Joint Secretariat set up as a result of that agreement and also secretary to the Environmental Impact Review Board. Also of assistance were Indian Affairs publications *The Western Arctic Claim: A Guide to the Inuvialuit Final Agreement* and *Western Arctic (Inuvialuit) Claim Implementation Annual Review 1988–89*.

I gained a good understanding of the James Bay Agreement by attending the conference, "James Bay and Northern Quebec: Ten Years After," held in Montreal in 1985 and sponsored by the Société de Recherches améridiennes au Québec. The published proceedings of that conference, *James Bay and Northern Quebec: Ten Years After*, were also most helpful. Quotations from the conference found in the Introduction and chapters 7 and 8 either come from my notes or from the published proceedings. Also of help in understanding developments in northern Quebec were pages 19–22 of *Completing Canada: Inuit Approaches to Self-Government*. Indian and Northern Affairs' 1982 review, "James Bay and Northern Quebec Agreement Implementation Review," was helpful in gaining the federal perspective on the agreement. Ian Cowie's *Future Issues of Jurisdiction and Coordination Between Aboriginal and Non-Aboriginal Governments*, especially pages 32–34, was most useful in understanding the operations of municipal government in northern Quebec. Phil Lancaster's master's thesis, "A Fiduciary Theory for Aboriginal Rights," advances the theory of federal and provincial liability in situations like the James Bay Agreement. Articles in the Montreal *Gazette* were useful in providing me with recent developments in Nunavik.

A number of sources were most helpful in gaining an understanding of the TFN agreement-in-principle. Those included Pauloosie Keeyutak, President of the Baffin Region Inuit Association, and Paul Quassa, at the time President of the TFN. Mr. Quassa was kind enough to meet with me on two occasions. Mr. Tom Molloy, chief federal negotiator, also was kind enough to talk to me about the agreement. Terry Fenge and Paul Okalik from TFN's Ottawa office told me about the negotiating process. Also of help was TFN's summary of the agreement, *Our Land Our Future*, and the supplements on the agreement which appeared in various issues of *Nunatsiaq News*.

Debra Rosin, Administration Officer of the Keewatin Inuit Association, and Percy Tutannuaq, Information Officer, talked to me about land claims, political development and social conditions as did Les Zettergren, Executive Director of the Kitikmeot Inuit Association. Mr. Peter Ittinuar, the first MP for the constituency of Nunatsiaq, provided me with his views on a variety of issues related to northern development.

Bernard Funston, Director, Constitutional Division, Department of Justice of the NWT was kind enough to talk to me about constitutional issues facing the north. Dan O'Neill, Assistant Regional Director of the Kitikmeot Region, and Roger Connelly, Regional Director for the Inuvik Region, provided me with information on the operations of the territorial government in the regions.

MLAs Peter Ernerk (who served until 1991) and Tony Whitford provided me with their views of constitutional development in the NWT.

Volume 5, Summer 1990 of *The Northern Review* gave me a good understanding of issue of devolution of power from the federal to the territorial government. Gurston Dacks's article, "Political and Constitutional Development in the Yukon and the Northwest Territories: The Influence of Devolution," was an excellent source of opinions on the effect of devolution on division.

Professor Bob Williamson, who spent many years in the north, was elected to the NWT council in 1966 and is now at the Anthropology Department of the University of Saskatchewan, was an excellent source of information on developments in the eastern Arctic and northern Quebec during the 1950s and 1960s.

Professor Howard McConnell from the College of Law, University of Saskatchewan, was kind enough to discuss current constitutional developments with me.

Sue Heron from the Dene/Métis Secretariat, Jack Williams, who worked with the Métis negotiating team and Faye Williams, Co-ordinator of the Métis Historical Association, all spoke to me about the Dene/Métis position on land claims and self-government.

Part III of Richard Diubaldo's work was particularly helpful in understanding the Quebec-Ottawa dispute over the Inuit.

While the struggle for Nunavut has been documented in many places, two written sources that were useful were Peter Jull's article, "Building Nunavut: A Story of Inuit Self-Government," and the book *Nunavut: Political Choices and Manifest Destiny* by John Merritt et al.

Saskatoon lawyer David Knoll told me about the statement of claim filed by his clients, the Dene of northern Saskatchewan, alleging that some of the Nunavut territory was in fact their treaty area and traditional Aboriginal land.

Statistics in the book come from four sources, unless indicated otherwise. Those are *Canada's North: The Reference Manual*; *Northwest Territories Data Book 1990/91*; *1990 Basic Departmental Data, Indian and Northern Affairs Canada*; and Statistics Canada (telephone reference service).

The full citation for printed items listed here is found in the Bibliography. Also listed are many other items that I read and relied on in preparing this manuscript.

Some of the material in Chapter 6 dealing with political, legal and constitutional developments appeared in slightly different form in my earlier book, *Our Land*. It has been revised so as to focus on the Inuit and has been updated to take into account recent developments. Some of the material in Chapter 8 dealing with the Métis comes from my book, *The Metis*. It too has been revised and updated. Both *Our Land* and *The Metis* were published by James Lorimer & Company as part of its Canadian Issues series.

Bibliography

General Reference

Canada's North: The Reference Manual. Ottawa: Indian and Northern Affairs Canada, 1988.

Northwest Territories Data Book 1990/91. Yellowknife: Outcrop, 1990.

1990 Basic Departmental Data, Indian and Northern Affairs Canada.

Books

Ames, Randy, Terry Fenge, Peter Jull, and John Merritt. *Nunavut, Political Choices and Manifest Destiny.* Ottawa: Canadian Arctic Resources Committee, 1989.

Bartlett, Richard H. *Indian Reserves and Aboriginal Lands in Canada: A Homeland.* Saskatoon: University of Saskatchewan Native Law Centre, 1990.

Berger, Thomas R. *Village Journey: The Report of the Alaska Native Review Commission.* New York: Hill and Wang, 1985.

Brody, Hugh. *The People's Land: Eskimos and Whites in the Eastern Arctic.* Markham, Ont.: Penguin Books, 1975.

Canadian Arctic Resources Committee. *Aboriginal Self-Government and Constitutional Reform: Setbacks, Opportunities and Arctic Experiences.* Ottawa: Canadian Arctic Resources Committee, 1988.

Coates, Kenneth. *Canada's Colonies: A History of the Yukon and the Northwest Territories.* Toronto: James Lorimer & Company, 1985.

Coates, Kenneth, and Judith Powell. *The Modern North.* Toronto: James Lorimer & Company, 1989.

Duffy, R. Quinn. *The Road to Nunavut.* Kingston and Montreal: McGill-Queen's University Press, 1988.

Fenge, Terry, and William E. Rees. *Hinterland or Homeland?* Ottawa: Canadian Arctic Resources Committee, 1987.

Grant, Shelagh D. *Sovereignty or Security? Government Policy in the Canadian North, 1936–1950.* Vancouver: University of British Columbia Press, 1988.

Griffiths, Franklyn, ed. *Politics of the Northwest Passage.* Kingston and Montreal: McGill-Queen's University Press, 1987.

Jenness, Diamond. *Indians of Canada.* 7th ed. Toronto: University of Toronto Press, 1977.

Keeping, Janet. *The Inuvialuit Final Agreement.* Calgary: The Canadian Institute of Resources Law, University of Calgary, 1989.

Lingard, C. Cecil. *Territorial Government in Canada: The Autonomy Question in the Old North-West Territories*. Toronto: University of Toronto Press, 1946.

Lyall, Ernie. *An Arctic Man*. Edmonton: Hurtig Publishers, 1979.

McGhee, Robert. *Canadian Arctic Prehistory*. Toronto: Van Nostrand Reinhold, 1977.

McMahon, Kevin. *Arctic Twilight*. Toronto: James Lorimer & Company, 1988.

Moyle, R. G. *British Law and Arctic Men*. Saskatoon: Western Producer Prairie Books, 1979.

Robertson, Gordon. *Northern Provinces: A Mistaken Goal*. Montreal: The Institute for Research on Public Policy, 1985.

The Town of Inuvik. *On Blue Ice: The Inuvik Adventure*. Yellowknife: Outcrop, 1983.

Chapters in Books

Cumming, Peter. "Canada's North and Native Rights." In *Aboriginal Peoples and the Law*, edited by Bradford W. Morse. Ottawa: Carleton University Press, 1985.

Lowe, Ronald. "Foreword." In *Kangiryuarmiut Uqauhingita Numiktittitdjutingit, Basic Kangiryuarmiut Eskimo Dictionary*. Inuvik: Committee for Original Peoples Entitlement, 1983.

McConnell, W. H. "The Meech Lake Accord." In *Meech Lake, Conflicting Views of the 1987 Constitutional Accord*, edited by Michael D. Behiels. Ottawa: University of Ottawa Press, 1989.

Moss, Wendy. "The Implementation of the James Bay and Northern Quebec Agreement." In *Aboriginal Peoples and the Law*, edited by Bradford W. Morse. Ottawa: Carleton University Press, 1985.

O'Keefe, Kevin. "Northwest Territories." In *Provincial and Territorial Legislatures in Canada*, edited by Gary Levy and Graham White. Toronto: University of Toronto Press, 1989.

Government Reports

Canada. *James Bay and Northern Quebec Agreement, and the Northeastern Quebec Agreement. Annual Report*. Ottawa: 1989.

Canada. House of Commons. Standing Committee on Aboriginal Affairs. *Unfinished Business: An Agenda for All Canadians in the 1990's*. Ottawa: March 1990.

Canada. Indian and Northern Affairs Canada. *Annual Report, 1989–1990*. Ottawa: 1990.

———*The Government of Canada and the Inuit, 1900–1967*. Ottawa: 1985.

———*In All Fairness, A Native Claims Policy*. Ottawa: 1981.

Canada. Indian and Northern Affairs Canada. *The Inuit*. Ottawa: 1986.

————*Inuit Land Use and Occupancy Project.* 3 vols. Ottawa: 1976.

————*James Bay and Northern Quebec Agreement Implementation Review.* Ottawa: 1982.

————*Living Treaties: Lasting Agreements.* Report of the Task Force to Review Comprehensive Claims Policy. Ottawa: 1985.

————*The 1987 Constitutional Accord.* Report of the Special Joint Committee of the Senate and the House of Commons, September 9, 1987. Ottawa: 1987. (Especially Chapter 12, "The Impact on the Northern Territories.")

————*Report on the Nature and Cost of the Transition to Nunavut.* Prepared by DPA Group for Indian and Northern Affairs Canada, October 1984.

————*The Western Arctic Claim: A Guide to the Inuvialuit Final Agreement.* Ottawa: 1984.

————*Western Arctic (Inuvialuit) Claim Implementation: 1988–89 Annual Report.* Ottawa.

Canada. Northern Science Research Group. *Eskimo Housing as Planned Culture Change.* Ottawa: Indian Affairs and Northern Development, 1972.

Irwin, Colin. *Lords of the Arctic: Wards of the State.* Ottawa: Health and Welfare Canada, 1988.

Newfoundland and Labrador. Intergovernmental Affairs Secretariat, Native Policy Unit. *Land Claims Policy.* St. John's: 1987.

Northwest Territories. *Directions for the 1990s.* Yellowknife: GNWT, 1988.

————*A Discussion Paper Prepared by the Government of the Northwest Territories on Political and Constitutional Development in the Northwest Territories.* 1988.

————*Financial Impact of Division.* Report prepared by Coopers & Lybrand for the GNWT, 1991.

————*1989 Annual Report.* Yellowknife: GNWT.

————*1990 Annual Report.* Yellowknife: GNWT.

————*A Position Paper on Political and Constitutional Development Presented by the Executive Council of the Government of the Northwest Territories to the Legislative Assembly.* February 25, 1991.

————*"Seize the Day," A Report to the Legislative Assembly on Political and Constitutional Development in the Northwest Territories.* GNWT, October 27, 1989.

————*Strength at Two Levels. A Report of the Project to Review the Operations and Structure of Northern Government.* November 1991.

————Legislative Assembly. *Division of the Northwest Territories; Administrative Structures for Nunavut.* Prepared by M. Whittington and Sheila MacPherson for the Sub-Committee on Division of the NWT Legislative Assembly, August 1983.

Northwest Territories. Legislative Assembly. *The Report of the Special Committee on Aboriginal Languages.* 1990.

——Legislative Assembly. *The Scone Report: Building Our Economic Future.* 1989.

Reports by Non-governmental Organizations

Canadian Arctic Resources Committee. "Future Imperfect." *Northern Perspectives* 17, no. 1. Ottawa.

Inuit Tapirisat of Canada. *Annual Report.* 1974–81, 1985–86, 1986–87, 1988–89.

——*Nunavut: A Proposal for the Settlement of Inuit Lands in the Northwest Territories.* February 27, 1976.

——*Political Development in Nunavut.* 1979.

IWIGIA. *Arctic Policy and Self-Determination: A Canadian Inuit Perspective, Indigenous Self-Development in the Americas.* Document 63. Copenhagen: July 1989.

Labrador Inuit Association. *Our Footprints Are Everywhere.* Nain, Labrador: 1977.

Nunavut Constitutional Forum. *Building Nunavut: A Discussion Paper Containing Proposals for an Arctic Constitution.* 1983.

——*Building Nunavut: Today and Tomorrow.* 1985.

——*Nunavut.* 1983.

——*Nunavut: Financial Perspectives.* Working Paper No. 2. 1983.

Société de Recherches amérindiennes au Québec. *James Bay and Northern Quebec: Ten Years After* (Forum Proceedings). Montreal: 1988.

Tungavik Federation of Nunavut. *Submission to the Task Force to Review Comprehensive Claims Policy by the Tungavik Federation of Nunavut.* September 27, 1985.

Western Constitutional Forum. *Chronology of Events: January, 1982–June, 1987.* Yellowknife: 1987.

——*Dene Government Past and Future.* Yellowknife: 1984.

——*Partners for the Future: A Selection of Papers Related to the Constitutional Development in the Western Northwest Territories.* Yellowknife: 1985.

Articles, Monographs and Position Papers

Arnold, Charles D. "Vanishing Villages of the Past; Rescue Archaeology in the Mackenzie Delta." *The Northern Review* no. 1 (Summer 1988): 40.

——"A Summary of the Prehistory of the Western Canadian Arctic." *Musk-Ox* 33 (1983):10.

Cowie, Ian B. *Future Issues of Jurisdiction and Coordination Between Aboriginal and Non-Aboriginal Governments.* Kingston: Institute of Intergovernmental Relations, Queen's University, 1987.

Dacks, Gurston. "The Case Against Dividing the Northwest Territories." *Canadian Public Policy* 12, no. 1 (1986): 202.

———"An Overview on Devolution." *The Northern Review* 5 (Summer 1990): 11

———"Political and Constitutional Development in the Yukon and Northwest Territories: The Influence of Devolution." *The Northern Review* 5 (Summer 1990): 102.

Funston, Bernard W. "Caught in a Seamless Web: The Northern Territories and the Meech Lake Accord." *The Northern Review* 3/4 (Summer/Winter 1989): 54.

Graham, Katherine. "Implementing Devolution: Learning from Experience." *The Northern Review* 5 (Summer 1990): 130.

Inuit Committee on National Issues. *Completing Canada: Inuit Approaches to Self-Government*. Kingston: Institute of Intergovernmental Relations, Queen's University, 1987.

Jull, Peter. "Building Nunavut: A Story of Inuit Self-Government." *The Northern Review* 1 (Summer 1988): 59.

Lester, Geoffrey S. *Inuit Territorial Rights in the Canadian Northwest Territories.* Ottawa: Tungavik Federation of Nunavut, 1984.

Lingard, C. C. "Administration of the Canadian Northland." *Canadian Journal of Economics and Political Science* 12, no. 1 (February 1946): 45.

Merritt, John, and Terry Fenge. "The Nunavut Land Claims Settlement: Emerging Issues in Law and Public Administration." *Queen's Law Journal* 15, no. 2 (1990): 255.

Nixon, P. G. "Early Administrative Developments in Fighting Tuberculosis among Canadian Inuit: Bringing State Institutions Back In." *The Northern Review* 2 (Winter 1988): 67.

O'Neil, John D. "Democratizing Health Services in the Northwest Territories: Is Devolution Having an Impact?" *The Northern Review* 5 (Summer 1990): 60.

Riewe, Roderick, Luke Suluk, and Lorraine Brandson. "Inuit Land Use and Occupancy in Northern Manitoba." *The Northern Review* 3/4 (Summer/Winter 1989): 85.

The Sustainable Development Research Group. *Coping with Cash.* Calgary: The Arctic Institute of North America, 1989.

Treude, Erhard. "Eighteenth Century Eskimo Land Cessions in Northern Labrador." *Musk-Ox* 26 (1980): 3.

Weller, Geoffrey R. "The Devolution of Authority for Health Care Services to the Governments of the Yukon and the Northwest Territories." *The Northern Review* 5 (Summer 1990): 37.

Lectures and Addresses

Clark, Joe. "Statement on Sovereignty." House of Commons. September 10, 1985.

Molloy, Tom. "Nunavut—The Land Claims Agreement in the Eastern Arctic: A Note of Optimism for Aboriginal Rights in the Summer of 1990." Saskatoon, October 4, 1990.

Suluk, Thomas. "Address to the 9th Legislative Council of the North-west Territories." February 22, 1980.

Thompson, Andrew. "Northern Land Claims Settlements: Contemporary Nation Building." Saskatoon, January 15, 1990.

Trudeau, Pierre Elliott. "Opening Remarks to the Federal-Provincial Conference on Aboriginal Rights." March 8, 1984.

Tungavik Federation of Nunavut. "Constitutional Future of the Northwest Territories." Presentation to the NWT Legislative Assembly, October 31, 1989.

Court Cases

Hamlet of Baker Lake v. Minister of Indian Affairs and Northern Development [1979] 3 Canadian Native Law Reporter 17.

Re Eskimos (Supreme Court of Canada) Vol. 5, Canadian Native Law Cases 123, also (1939) Supreme Court Reports 104.

La Commission Scolaire Kativik v. Procureur Général du Québec [1982] Canadian Native Law Reporter 54.

R. v. Tootalik (1970) 71 Western Weekly Reports 435.

R. v. Tootalik (1970) 74 Western Weekly Reports 740.

R. v. Sparrow (1990) 3 Canadian Native Law Reporter 160.

Land Claims Agreements

The Inuvialuit Final Agreement.

The James Bay and Northern Quebec Agreement.

Agreement in Principle between the Inuit of the Nunavut Settlement Area and Her Majesty in Right of Canada.

Dene/Métis Comprehensive Land Claim Agreement in Principle.

Council for Yukon Indians Comprehensive Land Claims Agreement in Principle.

Boundary and Constitutional Agreement for the Implementation of Division of the Northwest Territories between the Western Constitutional Forum and the Nunavut Constitutional Forum.

The Press

News stories in several publications were also of considerable help in researching this book. In particular I would like to mention:

Arctic Circle, published by Nortext in Iqaluit.

The Gazette, Montreal.

The special supplement dealing with Inuit in northern Quebec published by *Le Devoir*, April 1, 1989.

The Northwest Territories *Hansard*.

Nunatsiaq News, also published by Nortext.

The Press Independent, Denendeh's leading paper, published by D.M.
    Communications Ltd., Yellowknife.

Index